Sustainable & Kind

Traveler's Resource Directory

...for the generous, compassionate and respectful traveler.

C.J. Griffiths

*Travel Providers – Apps - Books– Podcasts – Magazines – Blogs - Technology
Terminology – Sustainable Packer – International Organizations*

Dedicated to the souls who venture into the world with a generous and compassionate heart – and to the companies, foundations, non-profits, scientists, writers, photographers, institutions and businesses who are dedicated to a sustainable future for the human family, animals, and planet.

C.J. Griffiths

INTRODUCTION

Sustainable & Kind Traveler's Resource Directory was developed as a one-stop shop to help travelers find life-enriching experiences in the world of eco-friendly and sustainable tourism.

There is a wealth of information and resources out there, so it can be a bit daunting to find just the right resource to plan that next great journey as a responsible traveler.

Planning a trip wisely with reputable providers focused on concerns like green accommodations, modes of transportation, tracking your carbon footprint, reducing waste, supporting the well-being of communities and wildlife can be challenging. Therefore, the criteria for the listings in the directory have been based on customer reviews and overall ratings.

We hope this directory will give you all the resources and tools you might need to inspire that next great adventure sustainably and with kindness for the planet, animals, and people.

"When one tugs at a single thing in nature, he finds it attached to the rest of the world."
– *John Muir*

"Wherever you go, go with all your heart."
– *Confucius*

"Take only memories, leave only footprints."
– *Chief Seattle*

TABLE OF CONTENTS

UN WORLD TOURISM ORGANIZATION
(UNWTO)

Tourism 2030 Agenda

A joint effort by UNWTO, UNDP and other partners, Tourism and the Sustainable Development Goals – Journey to 2030 aims to build knowledge and empower and inspire tourism stakeholders to take necessary action to accelerate the shift towards a more sustainable tourism sector by aligning policies, business operations and investments with the SDGs.

The bold agenda sets out a global framework to end extreme poverty, fight inequality and injustice, and fix climate change until 2030. Building on the historic Millennium Development Goals (MDGs), the ambitious set of 17 Sustainable Development Goals and 169 associated targets is people-centered, transformative, universal and integrated.

WHAT IS SUSTAINABLE TOURISM?

The goal of sustainable tourism is to minimize the negative impact on the environment and ensure that local communities benefit from tourism while preserving their cultural heritage for future generations. Sustainable tourism practices include using resources responsibly, reducing over-consumption and eliminating waste, preserving biodiversity, protecting native wildlife, and creating long-term socio-economic benefits for local communities.

Community
Engaging and working with local communities to ensure they benefit from tourism economically, preserves their environment, and protect their customs and traditions for the next generation.

Environment
Minimizing carbon footprint, reducing water consumption, using renewable energy sources, and protecting sensitive ecosystems.

Responsible Traveler
Encompasses ethical travel practices that consider environmental, economics, and social impact.

CHARACTERISTICS OF A SUSTINABLE TOURIST
- *Treads lightly, aware of the usage of resources and waste.*
- *Conscious of over-consumption.*
- *Respectful of biodiversity.*
- *Sensitive and respectful of the cultural heritage and traditions of the host community, and the economic impact of tourism on the communities future.*
- *Grateful for the self-enriching gift of travel!*

TYPES OF SUSTAINABLE TOURISM

Ecotourism

Ecotourism is a form of nature-oriented tourism intended to contribute to the conservation of the natural environment, generally defined as being minimally impactful, and including providing both contributions to conservation and environmental education. The Goal of eco-tourism is to encourage an appreciation for nature. Ecotourism provides financial incentives for the preservation and protection of delicate ecosystems, such as forests, coral reefs, and wildlife habitats.

Cultural Tourism

Cultural tourism often involves interacting with local communities, participating in traditional activities, festivals and supporting local artisans and craftsmen. By promoting cultural understanding and preservation, it contributes to the conservation of cultural heritage and promotes economic development in the local community. This form of tourism concentrates on immersing oneself in the culture, traditions, and heritage of a particular destination which also includes museums and historical sites.

Community-based Tourism

Community-based tourism involves the active participation of local people in planning, managing, and benefiting from tourism activities. It empowers local communities to preserve their natural and cultural assets, generate income, and improve their overall quality of life. Residents invite travelers to visit or stay in their communities or homes instead of a guesthouse, hotel or resort with the intent of providing an authentic experience of local culture and traditions. Involving local communities in tourism development encourages the preservation of natural resources, cultural heritage and helps minimize the negative impacts of tourism and ensures a viable future for the next generation.

Rural Tourism

UN Tourism understands Rural Tourism as "a type of tourism activity in which the visitor's experience is related to a wide range of products generally linked to nature-based activities, agriculture, rural lifestyle / culture, angling and sightseeing. Rural Tourism activities take place in non-urban (rural) areas with the following characteristics: 1) low population density, 2) landscape and land-use dominated by agriculture and forestry and 3) traditional social structure and lifestyle".

🌿 Geotourism

Geotourism is a form of natural area tourism that highlights features of the landscapes and geological attractions. It promotes tourism to geosites and the conservation of geo-diversity and an understanding of Earth Sciences through appreciation and learning. Geotourism is achieved through independent visits to geological sites, use of geo-trails and viewpoints, guided tours, geo-activities and patronage of geosite visitor centers. It provides opportunities for visitors to learn about the geological processes that shapes our planet and supports the conservation and safeguarding of geological sites.

🌿 Wildlife Tourism

Wildlife tourism can include safaris, birdwatching, snorkeling, and nature photography. Most wildlife tourism occurs in or around protected areas, such as nature reserves, national parks, and wilderness areas. Tourism also drives revenue to the protected areas themselves which helps finance their conservation and protection. "Wildlife tourism is a powerful tool countries can leverage to grow and diversify their economies while protecting their biodiversity and meeting several Sustainable Development Goals. It is also a way to engage tourists in wildlife conservation and inject money into local communities living closest to wildlife. Success stories and lessons learned from nature-based tourism are emerging from across the globe." *World Bank Group*

🌿 Volunteer Tourism

Volunteer tourism is booming, examples might include wildlife rehabilitation, environmental conservation like planting trees and beach cleanup, to helping a community build a school or dig a well. Being a responsible volunteer includes doing the research to ensure that those good intentions produce sustainably beneficial results. Tree Hugger's tips include researching organization's credentials, look at reviews, do they train volunteers, and void organizations that encourage handling of animals when it's not veterinary related, also look for projects that are run or managed by the local community.

🌿 *Slow Travel*

Slow travel encourages a thoughtful more drawn-out approach that focuses on an immersive experience and giving back to local communities. Examples might include taking the train instead of flying, engaging and visiting an artisan's workshop, taking a cooking class, visiting and exhibition at a museums or art gallery...meet the artist! Fast paced packed itineraries leads to single use plastics, overuse of fossil fuels, and a disconnect with culture or community. "More and more, travelers want to make real connections with local people, the place itself, and the local culture, and they're doing it by slowing their pace, avoiding the temptation to consume travel" - *Travlinmad*.

🌿 *Adventure Travel*

Adventure tourism involves challenging and often exhilarating outdoor activities like rock climbing, off the beaten track safaris, rafting, canoeing, off the trail hiking, trekking and camping. The sustainable approach to adventure tourism should be responsible and low impact so that it doesn't disturb the natural environment. It offers the adventurer the opportunities to connect with nature and develop a greater appreciation for the environmental and encourage a more proactive role in conservation movements.

🌿 *Agrotourism*

"...agritourism, which focuses on experiencing and understanding rural agricultural practices. It allows visitors to participate in farming activities, taste local produce, and learn about sustainable farming methods. Agritourism supports local farmers, stimulates the rural economy, and promotes sustainable practices in agriculture." – *NCESC.com. Agritourism invites visitors to connect with the land, experience rural life, and discover the origins of their food.*

Regenerative Tourism: Beyond Sustainability

"A growing trend within sustainable tourism is the shift towards regenerative tourism, a concept that goes beyond simply minimizing damage to the environment and instead focuses on actively restoring and enhancing ecosystems. Unlike traditional sustainable tourism, which aims to leave no trace, regenerative tourism encourages travelers and tourism businesses to give back to the environment. The goal of regenerative tourism is closely aligned with the principles of the circular economy which emphasizes reducing waste, reusing resources, and recycling materials. This approach ensures that tourism has a positive long-term impact on the environment." – *ECObnb.com*

Inclusive Tourism

The future of tourism is one that is accessible to all, including people with disabilities ensuring that public transport, and accommodations are accessible. "Accessibility for all to tourism facilities, products, and services should be a central part of any responsible and sustainable tourism policy. Accessibility is not only about human rights. It is a business opportunity for destinations and companies to embrace all visitors and enhance their revenues." – *UN Tourism*

Sustainable Tourism

DO THIS — NOT THAT

☑ Treat your HOTEL ROOM like it is your own HOME

☑ Know the LOCAL CUSTOMS and follow them

☑ Find out the real MONETARY VALUE of things and adhere to those prices

☑ Ask for permission before taking somebody's PHOTO

☑ Respect local TRADITIONS and RELIGION

☑ Learn some basic words and phrases in the local LANGUAGE

☑ Support the local shops and ARTISANS

☑ Report CHILD sex tourism

☒ Don't throw away or leave behind any EXPENDABLES that you brought

☒ Don't buy illegal WILDLIFE products and HERITAGE antiques

☒ Don't encourage BEGGING by giving money to paupers and STREET KIDS, rather donate to a local NGO

☒ Don't overly display your "first-world" GADGETS

☒ Don't be condescending or arrogant when TALKING to locals

☒ Don't JUDGE an entire culture based on a single individual

☒ Don't agree to BRIBE officials

☒ Don't LITTER, even if locals do

CONSIDER THIS

Offset your CARBON FOOTPRINT

Minimize air travel in favor of land or sea TRANSPORT

Join a local NGO or do some VOLUNTARY work
¬ learn how you can make a difference

Set a GOOD EXAMPLE for locals and fellow travelers
¬ how you behave will influence how locals see future travelers

Curb your FREEDOM of SPEECH about government and religion
¬ not doing so could get you and your local friends in serious trouble

Stay in family-run hotels/hostels or do a HOMESTAY

Carry REUSABLE CONTAINERS
¬ use them at street food and drink stalls instead of the disposable ones provided

"Take nothing but pictures. Leave nothing but footprints. Kill nothing but time."

Created by The Backpacker Spot©
www.thebackpackerspot.com

S&K
RECOMMENDED
BOOKS

S&K RECOMMENDED BOOKS

PLEASE NOTE: Many of the books being recommended may have additional outlets or channels for their writings like websites, blogs or podcasts, these will not be listed in those sections of the directory for the purpose of providing the traveler a wider selection of voices.

There is a world of books, guides and journals on travel from every conceivable experience, expertise and genre, S&K's recommendations are but a modest selection based on sustainable travel as a working principle, customer reviews, overall ratings within the community of responsible travelers and travel professionals. This basic criteria also applies to the other sections of the directory: websites, apps, blogs and podcasts.

The goal in selecting these recommendations is to provide the traveler with as many voices and perspectives as possible. There are remarkable and famous travel writers and TV personalities that many admire and follow as I do, so the S&K recommendations are focused on a particular aspect of travel, sustainability and the kindness along the journey.

CONSIDERATIONS: The recommended books were selected from the Amazon website but may also be available through their affiliates and other outlets!

ABOUT

This practical and inspiring guide, the latest in our popular Handbook series, motivates travelers to take a responsible approach to the impact of travelling. Whether you're looking to reduce your carbon emissions, enjoy more a responsible wildlife-watching experience, harness culinary tourism for good or enjoy an eco-friendly city break, this guide has got you covered. With top five and top ten lists discussing the best places to hike, volunteer, scuba dive and snorkel responsibly, as well as where to enjoy sustainable safaris, family trips and the best ways to give back when you travel, no stone is left unturned in this 168-page  guide to ethical tourism. Destinations discussed include relatively off-the-map regions of the world, including Guyana, Palau and Siargao in the Philippines, as well as more well-known places, such as Costa Rica, Uruguay and Jordan.

ABOUT

This is Lonely Planet's guide to the world's best eco-friendly resorts and experiences. From eco-lodges with cutting-edge sustainability initiatives to tours designed to protect wildlife and empower communities, you'll discover remarkable places where you can feel good about spending your time and money.
There are nearly 180 escapes to choose from, organized across five themes: Nature, Relaxation, Culture, Urban and Learning, to make it easy for you to find your perfect getaway - from tracking rare black rhinos in Namibia to a high-end private island hideaway in Indonesia, or a remastered heritage hotel in Monaco to an innovative community tourism project in Cuba.

Each escape is labelled with the key sustainability features you can enjoy while staying at the hotel or participating on the tour - whether it's wildlife spotting, sustainable dining, conservation opportunities, homestays, expert talks and more.

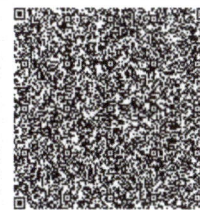

AUTHOR

Lonely Planet - With over 150 million guidebooks in print, Lonely Planet is a trusted source for any traveler. Since our inception in 1973, we've inspired generations of travelers to discover amazing places and enabled curious travelers to get off the beaten paths to appreciate different cultures and become agents of positive change.

ABOUT

Travel can be a blast, but there are hidden costs to your trips that go deeper than your pockets. From potential impacts on the environment or the communities we visit to respecting others' cultures, taking a moment to consider our choices can make a real impact on the planet and other people. Whether it's doing the research to make sure the money we pay to see wild animals isn't going into the pockets of those abusing them or forgoing the familiarity of Starbucks for local restaurants, there are countless ways we can travel more consciously. This book offers 100 tips to help protect the planet, support communities, and plan trips that are more mindful for anyone who wants to explore the world while conserving everything that makes it so special.

AUTHOR

Imogen Lepere - An award-winning travel writer based in London who specializes in food, female empowerment, and community. Her previous adventures include living with a commune on a Thai island, couch surfing around Scandinavia, riding the Trans-Mongolian Railway, sailing to Indonesia's Spice Islands, and that summer spent with a nudist colony in Greece.

ABOUT

A brilliantly evocative, surprising, and thrilling exploration of how tourism has shaped the world, for better and for worse—essential listening for anyone looking for a deeper understanding of the implications of their wanderlust. Through deep and perceptive dispatches from tourist spots around the globe—from Hawaii to Saudi Arabia, Amsterdam to Angkor Wat—The New Tourist lifts the veil on an industry that accounts for one in ten jobs worldwide and generates nearly ten percent of global GDP. How did a once-niche activity become the world's most important means of contact across cultures? When does tourism destroy the soul of a city, and when does it offer a place a new lease on life? Is "last chance tourism" prompting a powerful change in perspective, or driving places we love further into the ground?

AUTHOR

Paige McClanahan - A regular contributor to The New York Times reporting on the impacts of tourism. Her travel journalism has been recognized by The Society of American Travel Writers and the North American Travel Journalists Association.

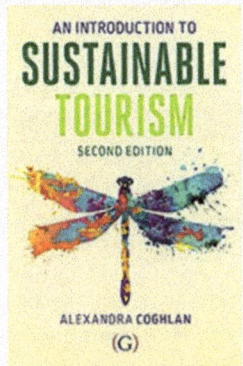

ABOUT

Fully revised and updated for a second edition, it provides a comprehensive, pragmatic, and realistic look at integrating sustainability into tourism. Includes two new chapters on regenerative tourism and disruptors including the impact of COVID-19 and new material on systems thinking, influencing behaviors and green marketing.

AUTHOR

Alexandra Coghlan - Associate Professor in Tourism at Griffith University in Queensland, Australia. She has worked primarily in sustainable tourism and nature-based tourism, with a strong focus on conservation and social and environmental benefits of tourism.

ABOUT

A comprehensive and realistic look at integrating sustainability into tourism.It adopts a systems-perspective and combines theoretical and applied knowledge with a scaffolded learning approach to take a comprehensive look at practical management tools, certifications and innovation to implementing sustainable tourism.

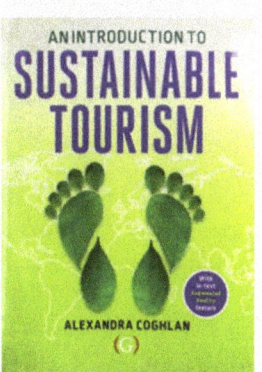

AUTHOR

Alexandra Coghlan - Associate Professor in Tourism at Griffith University in Queensland, Australia. She has worked primarily in the area of sustainable tourism and nature-based tourism, with a strong focus on conservation and social and environmental benefits of tourism.

ABOUT

Daniel shares his own tips as well as drawing on interviews with travel legends like Richard Branson, pros like Delta's longest serving flight attendant ever, and everyday folks with fascinating stories. You'll meet Kevan Chandler, a young man in a wheelchair who realized his dream of seeing Europe thanks to six friends who carried him around in a homemade backpack; Captain Lee Rosbach of Bravo's Below Deck, who guides his young crew to all ends of the earth; and Laura Dekker, the youngest person ever to sail single-handedly around the world. They talk about everything - from their favorite places and their worst misadventures to the environmental and economic impacts of travel. And everyone attests to how their cross-cultural experiences have shaped their worldviews, their politics, their relationships, and even their careers.

AUTHOR

Daniel Houghton - *The former CEO of renowned travel guide publisher Lonely Planet, a look at how travel can transform not only the traveler but also the world.*

ABOUT

The Bucket List is focused on sustainable travel featuring 1,000 vacation ideas that are eco-friendly, respectful of local cultures, and highlight opportunities to give back. A new era of sustainable travel is dawning – more than ever, vacationers are seeking experiences that are sustainable for the environment, sensitive of other cultures, make a positive impact, and above all, do no harm. Included are a diverse collection of sustainable travel ideas and eco-friendly destinations for all ages and interests. These experiences range from volunteering at a wildlife preserve or centering a foodie getaway around zero-waste to visiting the Eden Project, a series of biomes and

gardens in a reclaimed Cornwall mine designed to raise ecological awareness with educational programs and agriscaping.

AUTHOR

Juliet Kinsman - A Sustainability Editor at Condé Nast Traveler and regular contributor to The Times and The Telegraph. Author of Louis Vuitton City Guides, she also created Bouteco, a non-profit platform showcasing design-led hotels committed to sustainability.

ABOUT

It can be challenging to travel at your own pace in the modern world without falling for the temptations of fast planes, cheap airlines, last-minute tickets, quick-fix travel apps and overzealous tour operators. To take a back seat and allow yourself time to embrace the ebb and flow of travel requires a more thoughtful and philosophical way of journeying. Slow Travel: A Movement is a beautifully designed and practical compendium of places, activities, tours and experiences that will inspire you to get on the road in your own time and on your own terms. This book explores slow travel as a physical or philosophical endeavor, taking readers off the beaten track and through nature, and unveils journeys that will nurture talent and ignite the inner self. In this fast-paced world, it's worth adjusting your vacation time to a pace we can all strive to keep up with.

AUTHOR

Penny Watson - a trained journalist and award-winning travel writer with a serious case of wanderlust. She has traveled the world, written feature articles for countless magazines, newspapers and blogs, and researched a few guidebooks.

ABOUT

Bestselling vegan author and travel maestro Todd Sinclair has broken new ground with this pioneering look at the future of travel. Combining Sinclair's 15 years of travel expertise with thorough research and a careful consideration of vegan values, REBEL VEGAN TRAVEL GUIDE: Veganism on the Go is the first book to show how we can use the lessons of the pandemic to help us go back out into the world and connect more ethically and sustainably. Vegan travel is about compassion and sustainability. It's about being kinder to the planet, the animals, local communities and yourself.

AUTHOR

Juliet Kinsman - A Sustainability Editor at Condé Nast Traveler and regular contributor to The Times and The Telegraph. Author of Louis Vuitton City Guides, she also created Bouteco, a non-profit platform showcasing design-led hotels committed to sustainability.

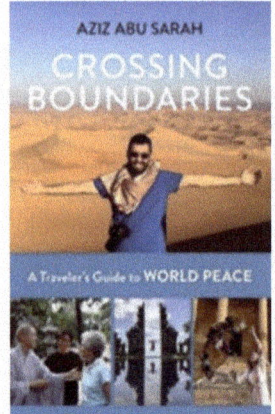

ABOUT

An essential strategy book for how to have transformative, sustainable, responsible travel experiences—starting at your own front door. Recognized Peacemaker and National Geographic Explorer Aziz Abu Sarah shows how, by crossing boundaries, we can heal our world from stereotypes, prejudice, and ignorance. Whether you're planning future travels or exploring the diverse cultures in your own community, Crossing Boundaries provides strategies for growth and getting out of your comfort zone. Moving between inspirational stories, humorous anecdotes, and helpful conflict resolution tips, Abu Sarah guides you through having personal, meaningful experiences with people from different backgrounds. He sketches a vision of a kind of travel with the power to help heal the divides of a world polarized by seemingly intractable conflicts. You'll discover shared values, build lasting relationships, and realize that, ultimately, far more unites us than divides us.

AUTHOR

Aziz Abu Sarah - A Palestinian peace activist, journalist, social entrepreneur and politician. He is the co-founder of the alternative tour company Mejdi with his Jewish friend Scott Cooper, which gives different perspectives on any given point of interest to tourists in various multi-cultural locales.

ABOUT

Gold Medal Winner: International Book Award in the Travel Category, 2017. Gold Medal Winner: Independent Press Award in the Travel Category, 2017. Silver Medal Winner: Reader's Favorite Award in the Travel Genre, 2017. "Making the world his friend, considering it a single country, and then distilling from years of first-hand experience a philosophy of travel, Nicos inspires and equips his readers not only to maximize the experience, but to maximize the value of the experience." – Rick Steves, Travel Writer and TV Presenter. "An epic journey with a master philosopher." – Daniel Klein, New York Times best-selling author

AUTHOR

Nicos Hadjicostis - Studied physics at King's College London then managed the largest media group in Cyprus over a decade. Leaving media, he traveled around the world for six-and-a-half years, exploring the world as if it were one huge country, a single destination that eventually inspired his book Destination Earth.

ABOUT

Sustainable Travel offers practical and achievable advice for those who want to make a difference in the way we experience the world, filled with great tips, tricks and ideas to help you explore the planet in a sustainable way! Having travelled around the world without flying, sustainability expert Holly Tuppen knows a thing or two about low-carbon and positive-impact adventures. Here, she shares what she's learnt from over a decade of responsible travels. Also included is a guide to regenerative travel experiences, including conservation-minded tours, community-led initiatives, alternative adventures, responsible destinations and green places to stay. A series of interviews feature the experts and unsung heroes of sustainable travel.

AUTHOR

Holly Tuppen - In 2008 she set off on an around-the-world-without-flying adventure. On her return, she began to spread the word about sustainable travel through marketing for Green Traveller and as editor of Green Hotelier. Currently a specialist in sustainable travel, creating content for The Long Run, the World Travel and Tourism Council, and the Association of British Travel Agents.

ABOUT

A pocket-sized guidebook to help us all become more aware of the impacts of our travel choices – both on the planet and on the local communities whose homes we are visiting – and to equip us with practical tips and advice on how to have more responsible, ethical and eco-friendly travels. The Responsible Traveller is your ticket to sustainable and ethical travel. Whether you travel out of curiosity, to find respite, to remind yourself of how vast and wonderful our planet is, or in search of life-shaping adventures, having the freedom to explore can be exhilarating and hugely rewarding. However, we owe it to the people, cultures, ecosystems and wildlife that we encounter along the way to travel with respect; to preserve our beautiful world for generations to come.

AUTHOR

Karen Edwards - A freelance editor and writer from London, who specializes in responsible tourism, sustainable living, well-being and music. She has written for a variety of national and international titles, including Adventure.com, High Life, Grazia, Metro, The Independent, The Telegraph and Time Out.

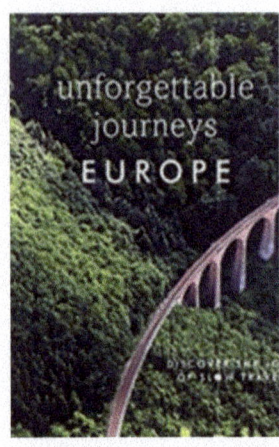

ABOUT

"The slower you go, the more treasures you'll uncover - so why would you want to rush the experience?" Featuring over 150 inspirational entries, Unforgettable Journeys Europe is a vibrant celebration of taking the scenic route. We've picked the best adventures across the continent, from cruising around the Western Fjords of Norway to hiking the Lycian Way in Turkey. Of course, the big-hitters are covered - riding Switzerland's Glacier Express, ferry-hopping in Greece and cycling from Land's End to John O'Groats - but we also take you off-the-beaten path, roaming the Albanian Riviera, kayaking through Finnish Lakeland and navigating the steady switchbacks of the Transfagarasan Road in Romania.

AUTHOR

*Luke Waterson -*Developed a penchant for travelling at an early age and following completion of an English Literature and Creative Writing degree at the University of East Anglia. Joseph Reaney – A freelance travel writer based in the UK and Czech Republic. He writes about Central and Eastern Europe for publishers like Lonely Planet, DK Eyewitness, Fodor's Travel, National Geographic and Rough Guide.

ABOUT

In this personal journey, ultra-light backpacker and sought-after speaker Glen Van Peski shares the life lessons he has learned through years of lightening his pack and helping others. Adventures provide the richness and texture to a life well lived. So, remain open. Keep saying "YES" to life's opportunities. In this book, you will discover transformative life lessons, which may go against the grain of popular thought but have been proven to change lives for the better. You'll learn that: Often the best strategy for achieving goals comes from subtracting rather than adding. When your first instinct is generosity, the long-term dividends will be greater than if you strive to gain your own advantage.

AUTHOR

Glen Van Peski - Ultra-light backpacker and sought-after speaker shares the life lessons he has learned through years of lightening his pack and helping others. Helped revolutionize backpacking by creating ultralight equipment, which allows people to take less so they can do more in the wilderness.

ABOUT

In a world obsessed with speed and ticking destinations off a list, The Art of Slow Travel invites you to embrace a different kind of journey— one rooted in genuine experience, discovery, and personal growth. Blending personal anecdotes, practical tips, and cultural insights, this book reveals how to fully immerse yourself in your surroundings, connect meaningfully with people and places, and cultivate mindfulness along the way. Whether you're staying a month or simply choosing to wander without a fixed itinerary, it walks you through how to organize and plan a slow journey in a step-by-step manner.

AUTHOR

Bhavana Gesota - An Indian American software technology veteran, a self-taught artist, and a meditator. Her professional life coupled with her own desire to explore the world since she was a child led to her living in nine countries, working in seven, and traveling to twenty-three more over five continents.

ABOUT

This sustainable travel handbook inspires readers to explore our fascinating planet without causing it further harm. Ten chapters help you go lightly, including how to choose the least impactful methods of travel, how best to protect wildlife, how to pack with more consideration and how to implement mindful practices into each travel day, Go Lightly gives the reader a tool kit of fresh ideas for travelling more consciously. The book also covers eco-friendly activities including biking, boating and camping, and introduces us to some of the world's most inspiring eco-adventure pioneers.

AUTHOR

Nina Karnikowski - Nina is based in the Australian surf town of Byron Bay. She writes travel stories for newspapers, magazines and websites, and has written about and travelled to over 60 countries. In response to climate change, she is now revolutionizing her practices.

ABOUT

Ever dreamed of walking the Camino de Santiago, driving Route 66 or riding the Trans-Siberian Railway? It may sound clichéd, but sometimes it really is all about the journey, rather than the destination and what better way to see the world than by moving through it. f setting out on an adventure is on your bucket list, but you don't know where to start, Unforgettable Journeys will have you lacing up your hiking boots, hitting the road or taking to the high seas. Encompassing everywhere from Antarctica to Zambia, over 200 hikes, drives, cycling trails, train routes and boat trips are brought to life with inspiring narrative, sumptuous photography and illustrative maps. We even suggest alternative routes, so it's easy to plan your next trip.

AUTHOR

Joseph Reaney - An experienced freelance travel writer based in the UK and Czech Republic. He writes about both, as well as the rest of Central and Eastern Europe (and beyond), for publishers like Lonely Planet, DK Eyewitness, Fodor's Travel, National Geographic and Rough Guide.

ABOUT

The invigorating true story of a man and his dog who circled the globe on foot. "Quietly stunning." — Laurie Woolever, New York Times bestselling author of World Travel with Anthony Bourdain and Bourdain: The Definitive Oral Biography. After the death of a close friend at seventeen, Tom Turcich resolved to make the most out of life; to travel and be forced into adventure; to experience and understand the world. On April 2nd, 2015, he set out to see it all — one step at a time. The World Walk is the emotional and exhilarating story of the tenth person and first dog to walk around the world. Together, Turcich and his dog, Savannah, covered twenty-eight thousand miles over the course of seven years

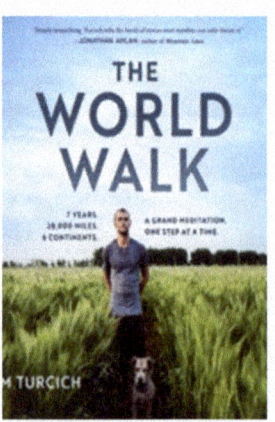

AUTHOR

Tom Turcich – Tom has been featured on CNN, Good Morning America, The Guardian, BBC, The Today Show, and more. Now a sought-after motivational speaker, Turcich inspires audiences with tales of perseverance, adventure, and the transformative power of pursuing one's dreams.

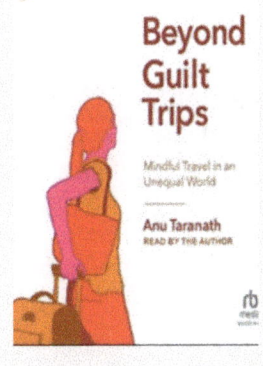

ABOUT

While travel abroad can provide much-needed perspective, it can also be deeply unsettling, confusing, and discomforting. In Beyond Guilt Trips: Mindful Travel in an Unequal World, storyteller Anu Taranath begins at home, unpacking our baggage about who we are, where we come from, and how much we have. She takes us on a journey through engaging personal travel stories and thought-provoking questions, providing us with tools to grapple with our discomfort and navigate differences with accountability and connection. Yes, travel! But be mindful. Be present. Beyond Guilt Trips: Mindful Travel in an Unequal World, was named as a Washington State Book Award Finalist, one of Fodor's Travels "13 Books to Inspire Your Travels," and selected as one of Oprah Magazine's "26 Best Travel Books.

AUTHOR

DR. Anu Taranath - Is an award-winning Fulbright scholar and academic. Dr. Anu has taught about global issues, race, gender, identity, and equity to thousands of students, presented at high-profile as well as more humble events, collaborated with social change agents and innovative thinkers around the world.

ABOUT

Find the best travel deals, skip the lines, pack like a pro, and enjoy the easiest trip of your life with this definitive guide to making your next getaway smoother than ever. Traveling is full of exciting new experiences and discoveries - but it can also be expensive, disorganized, and stressful if you don't know the insider tricks to make it simpler. Travel Hacks includes hundreds of expert guidelines, hacks, and DIYs for staying relaxed while you plan, book, pack, and travel to your next destination.

AUTHOR
Keith Bradford - *Owner and webmaster of Bradford Media, which publishes 1000 Life Hacks.*

ABOUT

Guidebooks are for tourists and self-help books are for internal journeys. But what about the personal growth that comes from travelling? Freeman Fung has experienced life in over thirty countries and believes that travelling is the ultimate fast track to personal growth and self-mastery. Travel to Transform is a self-development guide for anyone feeling stuck in mundane routines and looking to discover more in life. This travel memoir demonstrates how becoming a global citizen unleashes opportunities to transform your life holistically, from a state of surviving to a state of thriving.

AUTHOR

Freeman Fung - An international author, speaker, and certified life coach who has advocated new global citizenship at TEDx, Mindvalley, world tourism forums, and more. Originally from Hong Kong, he left home solo at age 19 to live in Romania for a Global Village project.

ABOUT

 "Zero Altitude follows Helen Coffey as she journeys as far as she can in the course of her job as a top travel journalist – all without getting on a single flight. Between trips by train, car, boat and bike, she meets climate experts and activists at the forefront of the burgeoning flight-free movement. Over the course of her travels, she discovers that keeping both feet on the ground is not only possible but that it can be an exhilarating opportunity for adventure." – *Goodreads*

AUTHOR
Helen Coffey - Helen is a travel editor of The Independent and the first travel editor of a national UK publication to go flight-free. She regularly appears as an expert contributor on travel-related stories for the BBC News channel, BBC Breakfast, BBC Radio 4 and LBC, among others. She lives in London and tweets @LenniCoffey

S&K
RECOMMENDED
TRAVEL APPS

S&K RECOMMENDED TRAVEL APPS

PLEASE NOTE: Not all companies or organizations have travel apps, so please refer to other sections of the directory for more in-depth choices for sustainable travel in booking, travel planning and volunteer opportunities.

S&K's featured apps in this section of the directory were selected based on sustainability as a key principle, customer reviews, and overall ratings within the community of responsible travelers and travel professionals.

Apps are a powerful pocket-sized tool that can help you make the right choices in creating an eco-friendly and responsible travel plan, and unforgettable journey! Using these apps can also plant trees, restore habitats, connect to local communities, connect to nature, reduce your carbon footprint...and find that next great vegan restaurant!

They can also raise awareness about lesser-known eco-conscious areas and activities and most importantly help reduce tourism's impact on the environment, habitat, wildlife, and well-being of communities.

Note, there are country specific sustainable tourism apps also (e.g. Thailand, Turkey, and the Himalayan Mountains), so check before you go!

CONSIDER: *There is a wealth of travel apps from familiar brands we all trust and use regularly, many of them now offer eco-friendly choices, so check before you book!*

Ecosia
www.ecosia.org

Plant trees with your searches and be climate active every day — The Ecosia community is tackling climate change, protecting wildlife, and collaborating with local communities around the world, planting the right trees in the right places. Get Ecosia's browser to start planting trees with your searches. Like other search engines, they make money through ads, but they use 100% of our profits for the planet. The Ecosia community has already planted 150 million trees in over 35 countries. With one download you can help tackle climate change while also protecting your privacy.

SEARCH AND PLANT A TREE

COMMUNITY IMPACT

FairTrip
www.fiartrip.org

The FairTrip app is a collaborative guide that helps travelers to find and share local and authentic places while having a positive social and economic impact on their visit. Any user can add new places in one tap, provided it meets the FairTrip criteria: Authentic, Green, Local, Social and Fair. Every FairTrip user is actually a potential guide. *"With FairTrip, we are reinventing the travel guide with a unique application that is more than just a travel guide, but also a social network to help people find authentic places away from mass tourism."* - Brian Corrieri, CEO FairTrip

 WANDER

Wander
www.wandertravelapp.com

Wander is a social network of passionate travelers meeting new friends along their journey. Solo travel can be a journey of self-discovery, but it can also be a bit challenging to tackle by yourself. Going solo does not have to mean going alone, the Wander network can help travelers connect with others around the world to make their adventure more exciting and expansive. Meet new friends along the way and create meaningful experiences, whether it be a simple latte in a café along the Champs Elysées, a hot air balloon ride in Cappadocia, Turkey.

RV MEETS LOCAL

Harvest Host
www.harvesthosts.com

Harvest Hosts is an application and online membership service that links individuals with self-contained RVs to picturesque locations where they can park overnight at no cost, including farms, breweries, and distilleries. The membership offers a distinctive chance to interact with remarkable small business proprietors, savor exquisite wine tastings, explore operational farms, and view impressive museum exhibits. It promotes sustainable RVing practices like washable dishes, water conservation, solar power, eco-friendly products, and LED lighting, encouraging members to reduce, reuse, recycle, and travel responsibly.

Hopper
www.wandertravelapp.com

Hopper has ranked #1 travel app in over 70 countries! When you book with Hopper they plant 2 trees for free on your behalf to help offset the carbon footprint of your travel all a part of the *Hopper Trees program.* Hopper is an accredited travel agency partnered with airlines, hotels, homes, and car rental providers across the globe, so you can feel confident you're booking the perfect vacation at the best price. Hopper analyzes over 30 billion price points in real-time so you'll never miss a deal.

FLY STAY PLANT A TREE

Hostelworld
www.hostelworld.com

HOSTELS

Hotelworld's mission is simple, help travelers find people to connect with. They are the leading global online travel agent focused on the hostel market. They have over sixteen thousand hostels in over 180 countries, 13.7 million reviews, and website and app that operates in 19 different languages. Over 60% of Hostelworld's customers are solo travellers so a few taps, a chat, and linkup with other travellers.

PackPoint
https://www.packpnt.com

Award-winning PackPoint is a smart packing app and packing list builder for any traveler. PackPoint will tell you what you need to pack based on length of your journey, weather at your destinations, and activities planned during the trip. *The Apple App Store's "Best New App" and featured in The Washington Post, BBC, LA Times, Lifehacker, Fast Company's Co.DESIGN, and The Next Web. "A Travel App That Practically Packs Your Bags For You".*

Skyscanner
Skyscanner
www.skyscanner.com

Search flight, hotel and car rental deals to anywhere in the world while you're on the move. Save time and money, compare and book with your favorite travel brands all in one place. No extra charges like booking fees, just the best prices. *The Telegraph "The only 20 travel apps you'll ever need"and the New York Times "App for traveler's dreaming of their next trip".*

Tripit
www.tripit.com

Award-winning travel organinizer Tripit creates comprehensive itineraries, syncs with your calendar, and helps you share plans with others. It shows transportation options based on where your'e staying, notes safe neighborhoods safety scores, and adds items like photos, QR codes and PDFs. Includes airport terminal maps, tracks your carbon footprint and shows offsets. *Featured in the New York Times, Forbes, Wall Street Journal, NBC, and Travel& Leisure.*

Worldpackers
http://www.worldpackers.com/

VOLUNTEER AND STAY

Worldpackers is the safest community to travel and volunteer with. They have 11 years of history connecting more than 3 million travelers with 18 different kinds of hosts in over 140 countries! They confirm trips, provide safeguards, connect hosts, provide transparency, the ability to chat with other travelers, give back and make a real impact. The Worldpackers Academy offers training on how to be a volunteer, daily eco projects certification, how to be self-aware, travel solo, and much more.

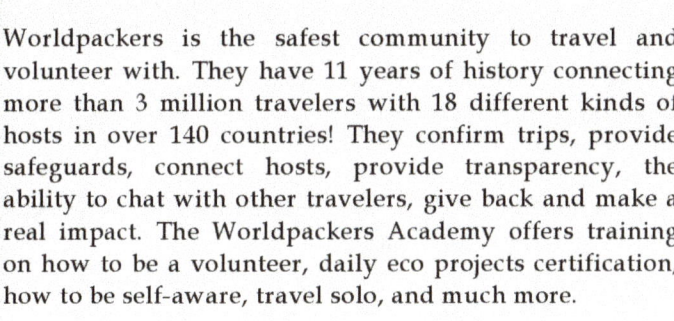

BlaBlaCar
www.blablacar.com

BlaBlaCar is a prominent community-based travel network with over 90 million members across 22 countries. It facilitates carpooling and bus travel, making transportation more affordable and eco-friendly. The network saves 1.6 million tons of CO_2 and fosters 120 million human connections annually. The concept originated in 2003 when the founder, struggling to get home, noticed many empty car seats during his journey! Statistics include 90 million members, 25 million travelers per quarter, and €1.4 billion saved by members since its inception.

Trainline
www.thetrainline.com

Train travel is a top choice for a responsible traveler. Trainline services millions of world-wide users and it's Europe's leading train and coach app. The app gives you live notifications on times, departures and arrival platforms, and updated departure times and prices on a monthly view calendar. With Trainline's Travel Journal you can discover city guides, inspirational journeys, compare prices and book. They offer thousands of options across 45 countries in Europe and the rest of the world.

LIME MICROMOBILITY
http://www.li.me//

Lime is dedicated to creating a future where transportation is shared, affordable, and carbon-free by offering short-term rentals of electric bikes and scooters in over 280 cities across nearly 30 countries. They aim to provide the most affordable, accessible, and equitable service in the industry, working closely with community organizations to address local needs. Through their Lime Hero program, riders can support community organizations by rounding up the cost of their rides. This initiative has raised over $500,000 globally for various non-profit causes. *Featured in Wired, The Verge, and The Standard.*

BIKE GLOBAL

Klima
https://www.klima.com

CARBON FOOTPRINT

Klima, an *Apple Design Award Finalist in 2021 and featured on Earth Day 2022*, is the leading application for immediate climate action. It enables users to calculate their carbon footprint and offset 100% of their CO_2e emissions within three minutes by supporting scientifically backed climate projects. Additionally, the app educates users on how to sustainably reduce their carbon footprint while monitoring their positive impact. Featured in *Forbes, TechCrunch, Wired, and Fast Company.*

FAIR FOOD FORAGER
https://fairfoodforager.com/

The Fair Food Forager app allows you to search ethical and sustainable food options using your location. Filter venues based on your needs, vegetarian, vegan, gluten free, home-made, or plant based. Fair Food Forager has over 6500 venues in more than 25 countries working on the principles of zero waste, self-sustaining living, a sense of community, clean seas, growing your own food, and supporting ecosystems.

EATWITH
http://www.eatwith.com/

BRING PEOPLE TOGETHER

Eatwith is the first global community providing shared food experiences by harnessing the relationship between food, people, cities around the world and spreading happiness through sharing. Their mission is to encourage people to engage in meaningful moments, immerse in nature, discovery cultures and celebrate family and friends believing we need to connect more today than ever. Their hosts are passionate about sharing their culture and providing you with a sense of community across the globe, so pull up a chair. *Featured in Vogue, Forbes, HuffPost, and Lonely Planet.*

HappyCow
www.happycow.net /

For over 25 years HappyCow has been the premier guide for locating exquisite plant-based and healthy dining options globally. With more than 240,000 listings across 185 countries, it facilitates the exploration of vegan and vegetarian cuisine. Users can find nearby restaurants, plan trips, and filter by various dietary preferences. The platform offers interactive maps, extensive reviews, and a community of over 1.2 million enabling users to connect, leave reviews, and share trips. The main app features are accessible in multiple languages including English, Spanish, French, German, Dutch, Italian, Japanese, Mandarin, and Cantonese.

VEGAN VEGETARIAN

Future Maps
https://future.coop/

FIND SUSTAINABLE EATS

Future Maps is a lifestyle app designed to help you discover great sustainable restaurants and cafés in your area. Whether you're craving vegan sushi, organic burgers, or gluten-free chocolate cake, Future Maps makes sustainable living easier and more attractive. One of the key features of Future Maps is its sustainability criteria. The app shows you the specific criteria that make each place a sustainability pioneer. *Vanilla Bean is now part of Future Maps.*

Tap Hydration & Waterstations
http://www.apps.apple.com/

Tap into a healthier and greener lifestyle with the Tap app, your go-to solution for finding water refill stations and tracking your hydration. With an extensive network of over 250,000 refill points sprawled across 100+ countries, including major cities like Los Angeles, New York, and London. Tap helps you ditch single-use plastic water bottles and embrace sustainability.

Localvore Passport
www.localvore.co

Localvore helps people discover restaurants, farmers, producers, and retailers who are sourcing locally, creating great food, and supporting their communities. The mission of localvore is to support local economies, promote sustainable food systems, and reduce food insecurity. Localvores believe that buying local food is better for the environment and for people. They currently only operate in the US with hopes of expanding overseas.

AllTrails
https://www.alltrails.com

AllTrails is a comprehensive guide and companion for outdoor activities such as hiking, biking, running, and walking. It offers detailed reviews and inspiration from a community of trail-goers and supports custom route planning for various needs, including dog-friendly and wheelchair-friendly trails. *Recognized as the number one best app of 2023 by Apple.* The company is committed to environmental conservation, contributing a portion of its membership fees to protect natural spaces and planting over 10,000 trees and counting. As a partner of Leave No Trace, AllTrails is dedicated to maintaining clean, safe, and respectful outdoor spaces.

HIKE - BIKE - RUN - WALK

Refill My Bottle
https://refillmybottle.com/

SOUTHEAST ASIA APP

Are you travelling to or living in South-East Asia? Download the new RefillMyBottle app to locate the closest water refill point, so you don't have to buy single-use plastic water bottles anymore. RefillMyBottle replaces the Refill Bali app, with new functionalities and more refill stations.

Citymapper
www.citymapper.com

Apple's App of the Year for five consecutive years, Citymapper is operational in numerous cities worldwide, assisting millions of commuters in their daily journeys. With extensive coverage in the US and Europe, the service is rapidly expanding to other metropolitan areas globally. Citymapper for Cities enhances transit systems by simplifying journey planning for users and providing transit agencies with tools and insights to optimize their networks. The app offers turn-by-turn directions for public transport, walking, cycling, and scooter trips.

CITY MAP PLAN

BikeMap
http://www.bikemap.net/

BIKE THE MAP

Bikemap provides an advanced route editor for planning cycling routes tailored to individual preferences, including options for road bikes, mountain bikes, and e-bikes. Users can choose from popular routes, smooth rides, or primarily cycling paths, and the editor adapts accordingly. With turn-by-turn navigation, users can explore surroundings and access over 14.3 million user-generated routes in more than 190 countries. The platform boasts over 9.1 million users who have created millions of unique routes, continuously improving the network through active community engagement and ongoing product development.

Rockd
https://rockd.org/

The Rockd app allows you to explore, learn and document your geologic surroundings as a professional or citizen scientist. Instant access to geologic and geographic summaries of your current location via a dashboard. Features include interactive global access to 290 geologic maps, 3D virtual globe, paleographic maps, and elevation data. Add your own field observations and use your phone compass to record geologic features and share with other users. Rockd is produced by the Department of Geoscience at the University of Wisconsin - Madison. Support provided by the National Science Foundation (NSF) and the Dept. of Geoscience.

CityMaps2go
www.citymaps2go.com

CityMaps2Go is the ultimate offline map for travelers, mountain biking, and hiking enthusiasts offering detailed maps of remote areas and national parks with terrain features available both online and offline. The app provides comprehensive content, including photos, tips, and detailed information for millions of locations worldwide. It covers over 150 countries and 60,000 destinations, functioning offline to avoid connectivity issues and data roaming charges. Users can plan trips, create lists, and share travel plans with friends, with the ability to sync across multiple devices. Praised by *Time Magazine*, *WSJ*, and *Macworld* for its utility and cost-saving features.

Komoot
www.komoot.com

Komoot offers advanced route planning and turn-by-turn voice navigation for outdoor activities such as hiking, mountain biking, road cycling, and cycling. Its features work offline, ensuring users stay on course even without a signal. With over 40 million users, the platform inspires community sharing through content-rich feeds of unique stories and adventures. Founded in 2010 by six friends from Germany and the Austrian Alps, Komoot now employs over 100 people dedicated to enabling great outdoor adventures.

HIKE RIDE 3D VIDEO MEMORIES

Relive
http://www.relive.cc/

Apple Apps Editor's Choice, Relive is an app that allows users to create 3D video stories of their outdoor activities such as running, cycling, hiking, skiing, and snowboarding. Users can track your activities, take photos, and share those experiences with friends on social media platforms. Video stories work with various apps like Suunto, Apple Health, Garmin Connect, Polar, MapMyRide, MapMyRun, MapMyHike and MapMyWalk. Relive offers a free version and a subscription-based Relive Plus, which includes additional features like adding music and up to 50 photos to videos. Hike and ride memories, 3dvideos , tag moments you care about, track your activity.

Wikiloc
www.wikiloc.com

Wikiloc offers a comprehensive platform for exploring and recording outdoor trails, supporting activities such as hiking, running, biking, kayaking, and skiing. Users can create and share custom maps, add photos, and access millions of trails worldwide. The app provides free offline topographic maps, turning smartphones into GPS navigators with real-time guidance and alerts. Additionally, users can share their location with family and friends, download trails to compatible devices, and access weather forecasts. A premium subscription supports environmental protection through a *contribution to 1% for the Planet.*

Autio
www.autio.com

Autio is a platform offering over 23,000 location-based audio stories narrated by well-known personalities such as Kevin Costner, Phil Jackson, and John Lithgow. These professionally edited stories provide a unique, multi-dimensional perspective on the landscape, its people, and its history as you travel. Autio has been featured in *Forbes, Outside, NBC, Southern Living, New York Times, Travel+Leisure,* and *Lonely Planet* to name a few. *"Autio could be the biggest thing I've ever been a part of."* – Co-Founder Kevin Costner

Culture Trip
www.theculturetrip.com

Award-winning Culture Trip's recommendations are hand-picked by a global community of travel experts and local insiders. The app gives you stories for an insiders perspective of destinations around the world, with lesser-known gems and the unexpected. They put local people at the center of their trips. provides income and benefits to the community, and connects you with the people, their traditions, and culture. *Featured in U.S. New, New York Times, Bella, Travel+Leisure, Traveller, and Metro.*

Day One Journal
http://www.dayoneapp.com/

Award-winning Day One redefines journaling! With over 15 million downloads and 200,000 5-star ratings globally. Day One has reinvented journaling with rich text, unlimited text entries, ability to create different journals within a day, add drawings, photos, and dictated audio - wherever you are or whenever you want. Apple App of The Year Editor's Choice, design award. "It feels almost sacred: A completely private digital space"- New York Times. *Also featured in Time, The Verge, The Washington Post, Lifehacker, and Wired.*

Polarsteps
http://www.polarsteps.com/

Over 10 million explorers have chosen Polarsteps to plan, track and relive their travels. This all-in-one travel app shows you the world's most enticing travel destinations, gives you insider tips, plots your route, gives you location and photos once your journey is underway. The result is a beautiful digital world map unique to you and a chance to turn it into a travel book. Polarsteps' Guides, created by other explorers like you, show you the best of the world as well as top tips once you get there. *"The Polarsteps app replaces your travel journal, making it easier and more beautiful."* - National Geographic

Travel Diaries
http://www.traveldiariesapp.com/

With 200,000 users and 15,000 books and counting, Travel Diaries offers a travel journal, book creator, travel tracker, and map maker. Users can create travel log books with itineraries, photos, maps, and keepsakes, and share their experiences on a webpage. The app also allows users to plan their next trips by mapping out countries, cities, and bucket list ideas. Travel Diaries' offers customizable layouts, fonts, and the ability to add photos and maps, making it easy to create a personalized travel journal that can be accessed seamlessly on both mobile and web platforms. *As seen on National Geographic, The Boston Globe, Metro, EMERCE, and de Volkskrant.*

Earth 3D Map
http://www.earth3dmap.com/L

Discover fascinating facts and useful information on Earth 3D Map's user-friendly interactive 3D globe app with beautiful graphics of physical and political maps, wonders of the world and updated global weather. Other features include topographic models of earth, physical maps, day/night cycles, time zones, 2,600 geographic objects and 500 wonders of the world. Add-ons include human world, animal world, plant world, and sky map. No internet required - five star ratings from users!

Withlocals
www.withlocals.com

Withlocals is a global community of locals and travelers who share a passion for travel and a desire to connect with each other, 1200 plus tours are available in over 70 cities in Europe and Asia. The app helps you book and connect with local hosts who will guide you personally - discover Rome bite by bite on a delicious tastings tour, or floating markets in the heart of Bangkok, or the hidden gems of Lisbon without the touristy crowds. "Connecting people and cultures is the very essence of humanity. It is through these connections that we can learn from one another, grow together, and build a better world for all." - Willem, founder of Withlocals

Marine Debris Tracker
http://www.debristracker.org/L

Join Debris Tracker in creating a bigger picture of the plastic pollution crisis by using the app to report litter wherever you find it, from our oceans to your backyard. Every day, dedicated educational, non-profit, and scientific organizations and passionate citizen scientists from all around the world use the Debris Tracker app to record GPS data on inland and marine debris. To date, Debris Tracker users have contributed 2 million items to our open-data platform, hosted at the University of Georgia. Together you help create a comprehensive understanding of marine debris and plastic pollution by collecting and sharing data, generating scientific findings, informing policy, and inspiring upstream solutions.

iNaturalist
https://www.inaturalist.org

The iNaturalist free app enables a community of nature lovers to document and disseminate their observations of flora and fauna - initated by *California Academy of Sciences and the National Geographic Society*. The application permits users to capture images of plants and animals and upload them to the iNaturalist website. It has been utilized in various research endeavors, including studies on avian migration patterns and plant phenology. The app promotes engagement from a diverse group of nature enthusiasts, such as hikers, hunters, birdwatchers, beachcombers, mushroom foragers, park rangers, ecologists, and fishermen..

Merlin Bird
https://merlin.allaboutbirds.org/

The Cornell Lab of Ornithology's mission is to interpret and conserve the Earth's biological diversity through research, education, and citizen science focused on birds and nature. Merlin Bird ID helps you identify birds you see and hear. Merlin is unlike any other bird app—it's powered by eBird, the world's largest database of bird sightings, sounds, and photos. Answer a few simple questions, upload a photo, record a singing bird, or explore birds in a region. Build and customize your own personal lists of bird sitings based on where you travel anywhere in the world.

Google Translate
https://translate.google.com/

Google Translate instantly translates text in over 100 languages, see a sign or a menu open app, point your camera text is translated instantly. Google Translate also lets you have conversations with people who speak different languages and download languages for offline use. This is especially handy when you're traveling and don't want to rack up roaming charges or can't access Wi-Fi. Just download the languages you need beforehand, no internet, no problem. There is also a conversation mode where you can talk into your phone in your language, and it speaks out the translation in the other person's language.

Waygo
http://www.apple.com/

Award-winning *Waygo* is a leader in visual translation services, your offline travel translator and dictionary app for Chinese, Japanese and Korean. Their technology allows you to hover your phone's camera over foreign text and instantly translate and read that text in English. Featured in *The New York Times, Los Angeles Times, ABC News, Discovery Channel and Popular Science.* "That's actually amazing."- BBC The Travel Show.

STARS AND PLANETS

Skysafari
http://www.skysafariastronomy.com/

Skysafari is a community based social stargazing app with three levels of subscriptions. All levels show best-known star clusters, nebulae, and galaxies including the Solar System's major planets and moons, and more than 200 asteroids, comets, and satellites. Upgrades offer more stars, asteroids, comets, deeper sky objects and state of the art mobile telescope control. *Featured in Common Sense Media, CNET, Astronomy Technology Today, Excellent Webworld, and podcaster Dave Farina (CosmosSafari.com)*

XE Currency
www.xe.com

The top rated Xe Currency app has everything you need for global money transfers and currency conversion. Converts currencies, checks live rates and news feeds, and transfers money securely with complete fee transparency. One of the key features of any currency converter, especially when traveling, is the ability to access rates while you are offline. Xe Currency enables fast, reliable money transfers in over 65 currencies to over 170 countries and pulls currency data in real time from over one hundred data sources, including trusted international banks, governments, and institutional investors.

Signal
www.signal.org

Signal is a state-of-the-art end-to-end encryption app that keeps messaging private. Signal is an independent nonprofit so there are no ads, no affiliate marketers, and no creepy tracking, so speak freely. Development is supported by grants and donations from people like you. Cyber experts are urging smartphone users to switch to fully secured platforms like Signal. "Signal is generally considered the most secure messaging app in existence." - Cyber Insider

S&K
RECOMMENDED
TRAVEL PROVIDERS

S&K RECOMMENDED TRAVEL PROVIDERS

PLEASE NOTE: Many websites have blogs, podcasts, magazines, and apps that may not have been included in the previous App section. In the Media section of the directory there are more in-depth recommendations of bloggers, podcasters, and magazines that are in addition to the websites.

There are amazing companies offering remarkable adventures around the world, but as with the Apps, the same criteria was used in the website recommendations: sustainability as a working principle, customer reviews, and overall ratings and feedback within the community of responsible travelers. *Many apologies to those we might have missed, it's a quickly growing community of committed companies...and it's a big world out there!*

What is B Corp certification? Many travelers today are aware of and look for B Corp certification when booking travel, you will notice most of the companies recommended are certified or are in the process of being certified. "B" means beneficial and *B Lab Global* is the certificating entity. They define a B Corp as a company's environmental and social impact. *"Certified B Corporations are leaders in the global movement for an inclusive, equitable, and regenerative economy"* - for more in depth information and understanding go to www.bcorporation.net.

CONSIDER: In many cases it was a fine line in selecting the recommendations for the directory as many travel companies are now committing to sustainable practices which is exciting, so next time you're on one of your favorite booking sites check their partnerships and sustainability policies and book accordingly!

BOOK - STAY - ADVENTURE ON

Above Safaris
http://www.abovesafaris.com

Above Safaris promotes sustainable travel in Tanzania, supporting local communities and innovation. Founded by a social entrepreneur with over a decade of experience, they offer high-quality, impact-driven travel experiences. *Featured experiences: Great Migration, trekking Kilimanjaro and yoga retreats.* The desire to do travel differently started with a responsible and sustainable approach, impact-driven travel without sacrificing the quality.

Amazonas Explorer
http://www.amazonas-explorer.com/

Since 1985 Amazonas Explorer has been Peru's adventure travel experts specializing in tours to Machu Picchu and the Amazon - follow Inca trails, trek Machu Picchu, or immerse in the cultural. They were the first Peruvian travel company to be B Corp certified, they are also members of the *1% for the Planet, and The Long Run* a sustainable travel movement. They also work with a Peruvian-based company Regenera in carbon offsets in the Manu National Park. *"The best adventure outfitters in Cusco" - Condé Nast Traveller*

& BEYOND
www.andbeyond.com

Award-winning &BEYOND, established in 1991, operates in sub-Saharan Africa, Asia, South America, and Antarctica, believing that travel has the power to transform. Their core ethic revolves around Care of Land, Care of Wildlife, and Care of People, aiming to leave the world a better place through conservation and extraordinary guest experiences. *Condé Nast Traveller Readers' Choice Award 2024.*

Agriturismo.it

Agriturismo
www.agriturismo.it

Agriturismo is *Italy's first website for booking farmhouses*, offering over 4500 rural accommodations such as houses, farms, cottages and more in various scenic locations. For over 20 years Agriturismo has connected location managers and farmers with tourists, promoting holidays that explore nature, ancient farming methods, and helping visitors discover the authentic culture of Italy and reconnect with nature.

Aracari
www.aracari.com

Award-winning Aracari has been leading the way in authentic and sustainable luxury travel in South America for over 20 years. They work with top local guides and travel experts from their Lima office to offer clients unforgettable experiences in art, culture, history, cuisine, and the outdoors. *Condé Nast Travellers' Top Travel Specialists 2025.*

Atlas Obscura
http://www.atlasobscura.com/adventures

Atlas Obscura has created a global community of travelers eager to explore the world's hidden gems. Since 2016, they've hosted small-group trips to amazing places, like swimming with sea turtles in the Galapagos or checking out Egypt's Valley of the Kings after hours. *Partnering with Intrepid,* they ensure their adventures are both responsible and purposeful. *"Well-known for award-winning journalism and building the definitive, community-driven guide to the world's hidden wonders..."* Atlas Obscura

Blue Yonder
www.theblueyonder.com

The Blue Yonder offers a variety of tailored getaways, from short trips to longer stays, including unique experiences like traditional puppetry, heritage trails, sleeping in a rainforest or waking in a luxury hotel. Their 2024 Sustainability Policy emphasizes responsible tourism, supporting local communities, fair labor, minimizing environmental impact, and preserving cultural heritage. *Partnered with Resilient Destinations Foundation that brings tourism development and humanitarian sectors together.*

Byway

Byway
http://www.byway.travel/

Award-winning Byway is a 100% flight-free travel platform that uses innovative routing technology to create enjoyable trips by land and sea, aiming to make travel more sustainable and fun. They highlight that rail travel produces significantly less CO_2 compared to air travel, emphasizing the need to reduce reliance on flights to benefit the planet. Travel by land, soak up the countryside, and stay wonderfully.

Cheesmans Ecology Safaris
https://cheesemans.com/

Cheesemans' Ecology Safaris has been organizing wildlife trips for over 40 years. They focus on sustainability and conservation, with a motto of *"Experience, Learn, Protect."* Since 2022, they've been carbon-neutral by working with carbon offset projects. *Their work has been featured in National Geographic Traveller (UK).*

THE WORLD IN CONTEXT

Context
http://www.contexttravel.com/

Context is a group of experts who encourage travelers to explore the authentic life, history, and culture of major cities. They are a Certified B Corp since 2011 and believe travel should protect rather than harm destinations. *Recognized by The Guardian, New York Times, Travel+Leisure, National Geographic, and Wall Street Journal.*

EcoCamp Pategonia
http://www.ecocamp.travel/

EcoCamp, run by Chilean tour operator Cascada Expediciones, offers top adventure trips in Patagonia and beyond. Founded in 1991 by friends Yerko Ivelic, Javier Lopez, and environmental steward Nani Astorga, Cascada has been providing eco-friendly adventures for over 25 years. Activities include trekking, mountaineering, and wildlife observation, attracting over 30,000 visitors to Chile. *Committed to social and cultural preservation and a working green ethos.*

experience TRAVEL GROUP
https://www.experiencetravelgroup.com/

ETG has always focused on sustainable travel and is B Corp Certified. They believe responsible travel can be a force for good. Every trip with ETG promises quality, responsible, and sustainable travel. They've been featured in *Condé Nast Travellers' Top Traveller', National Geographic, The Times, The Guardian, Wanderlust, and Family Traveller.*

TRAVEL WITH SOUL

When you travel with Fair Voyage, you know you're getting a fair and wonderful experience with non-negotiable values of humanity, peace and sustainability at the core of their working philosophy. Consistently rated 5 out of 5 by travelers, you know your money is making the world a better place. The team sources destinations that benefit the local communities and minimize your footprint. *As featured in Travel Weekly, Swiss Entrepreneurs Magazine, Sustainable Leaders, The Sunday Times, and Innovators.*

Fernweh Fair Travel
www.fernweh-travel.com

WOMEN OF THE HIMALAYAS

Award-winning Fernweh Fair Travel is *a women-led empowerment* project that offers guided tours in the Indian Himalayas. They mix nature adventures, spiritual retreats, and cultural activities. Guests stay in unique places like forest huts and boutique hotels. Their programs aim to educate and transform travelers while supporting local communities. *Featured in New York Times, National Geographic, DER SPIEGEL, ELLE, Adventure Travel News, Women's day and influencers like ThirdEyeMom.com.*

ITALY & BEYOND

Food.Stories.Travel
http://www.foodstoriestravel.com/

Food.Stories.Travel. designs and guides active vacations focused on connecting people with new places, cultures, and foods. They support local farmers and artisans, promote food entrepreneurs, and contribute to food-literacy organizations like Slow Food that supports food justice and environmental stewardship. *Featured in Belmont Voice, The Aspen Times, Ambassador Magazine, Bostoniano magazine, and Slow Food USA blog.*

G Adventures
http://www.gadventures.com/

GOOD TRAVEL & FAMILY

G for Good stands for all of the social, environmental and ethical good they create as a business which helps to fuel Community Tourism. A small group travel leader with a 30+ year history, dedicated to making travel a positive force. They focus on sustainability and creating a positive impact in the communities they visit. *G Adventures has partnered with National Geographic Family Journeys.*

Go Eat Give, a nonprofit started in Atlanta in 2011 is all about promoting cultural awareness through travel experiences. They offer unique trips like luxury farm stays in Tuscany, mezcal classes in Oaxaca, and volunteering in India. Their goal is to create meaningful and sustainable travel adventures. As seen on *CNN, USA Today, CBS, NBC, ABC and Telemundo.*

Gondwana Ecotours
www.gondwanaecotours.com

PASSIONATE TRAVEL

Gondwana Ecotours is passionate about sustainable travel with a softer footprint and carbon neutral tours. They offer tours that are kind to the environment, work with local businesses, and support local causes. Join them for adventures like seeing the Northern Lights in Alaska, visiting gorillas in Rwanda, or enjoying a BBQ in Patagonia. *Featured in New York Times, Chicago Tribune, Cooler, Forbes, The International Ecotourism Society, and Los Angeles Times.*

Human Connections
https://humanconnections.org/about

Human Connections, based in Bucerías, Mexico, is a non-profit that links local folks with international visitors through travel and experiences. They aim to empower communities and promote understanding. By working with Mexican artisans and tradespeople, they create real, meaningful exchanges where locals can share their culture and earn more, while travelers get a better understanding of Mexican culture. *Volunteers welcome and student programs are available!*

Intredpid
www.intrepidtravel.com

For over 30 years award-winning Inrepid has been creating unforgettable adventures with a mission to make travel a positive force, respecting local cultures and giving back through The Intrepid Foundation.For over 20 years The Intrepid Foundation, has been giving Intrepid travellers a chance to make a bigger impact in the places they visit, together they raised more than $15.5 million and supported over 160 communities around the world. *Intrepid Travel won the top award at the 2024 National Travel Industry Awards (NTIA) held in Sydney.*

.

Invisible Cities
www.invible-cities.org

Award-winning Invisible Cities is a social enterprise that trains people affected by homelessness to become tour guides in their own city, offering unique tours to both tourists and locals. Their high quality training empowers our guides to create, craft and deliver tours that are their own, highlighting monuments, people and places they have chosen themselves. *Lonely Planet's Best in Travel Community Award.*

RARE EXPEDITIONS

Joro Experiances
http://www.joroexperiences.com/

"Travel is a fundamental human desire, but if we want to see the world, we have to understand our responsibility towards it. And acknowledge there's more work that needs to be done." In 2021 Joro was the first luxury travel company to be a certified B Corp,founding members of The Conscious Travel Foundation and partner with Expedition Science that facilitates research and conservation efforts. Joro will introduce you to rare and exceptional travel worldwide, you'll experience pioneering conservation and community projects while minimizing your impact on the local ecosystem. Featured in Condé Nast Traveller, Brummell Magazine, Luxury Travel Magazine, and Elite Traveler.

Journeys With Purpose
www.journeyswithpurpose.org/

Award-winning Journeys With Purpose provides immersive travel experiences led by conservationists to promote global nature conservation projects. Their *"Seven Worlds, One Planet"* curriculum aims to restore biodiversity across all continents, with a commitment to a nature-positive, climate-resilient goal by 2030. As a mission-driven organization, their journeys are designed to be transformative for both travelers and the communities they visit, fostering a deeper engagement with cultures, wildlife, and landscapes. *Selected as an Earth Shot Nominator established by Prince William and The Royal Foundation.*

Kind Traveler
http://www.kindtraveler.com/

Kind Traveler "we believe that the heart that loves travel is the heart that can create meaningful change—for people, animals, and the environment". They work with over 400 hotels, destinations, and charities in 25 countries, helping travelers give back to local communities. Testimonial examples include *Condé Nast Traveller, NBC, Travel & Adventure Show, and Animal Defense Fund.*

**National Geographic- Lindblad
Expeditions
www.expeditions.com**

For over fifty years, *Award-winning* National Geographic-Lindblad Expeditions has been dedicated to environmental care and responsible exploration, with a core belief that enhanced knowledge increases our understanding of our role in protecting natural and cultural treasures. They offer a 100 itineraries across seven continents relying on a fleet of exceptionally advanced ships built small and nimble in order to venture into more remote places. *Voted one of the 10 best Intimate-Ship Ocean Cruise Lines in 2024 Travel+Leisure* World's Best Awards.

Lokal
www.lokaltravel.com

Watch the *award-winning documentary film 2.5% The OSA Peninsula* that inspired Lokal. Lokal offers customized adventures that let you dive into local cultures, support communities, and protect the environment. You can stay in eco-friendly lodges, learn from local guides, and enjoy home-cooked meals. By traveling with Lokal, your money directly benefits the communities you visit. Lokal aims to ensure fair distribution of tourism revenue, promote sustainable practices, and uplift the unique qualities of each destination. *As featured in New York Times, National Geographic, Lonely Planet, CNN, Vogue, and Impact Travel Alliance.*

Much Better Adventures
http://www.muchbetteradventures.com/

Much Better Adventures partners with independent businesses to eliminate middlemen and maximize the local economic impact of travel spending. Their model directs 76% of every $100 spent into local economies, creating jobs and sustainable livelihoods in rural areas, which aids conservation efforts. Additionally, 5% of their revenues support the World Land Trust's Buy an Acre program, helping local communities purchase and protect natural habitats. *"One of the best travel companies committed to climate action"* -The Guardian.

Natural Habitat Adventures
www.nathab.com

Award-winning Natural Habitat Adventures is all about conservation through exploration. They teamed up with World Wildlife Fund to create unique trips to remote places, aiming to protect the planet and support local communities. Awarded *World's Best Travel Company by Outside, Travel+Leisure's Top Tour Operator, and Newsweek's Best Adventure Travel Company.*

Nature Travels is about protecting nature and promoting responsible tourism. *They partner with organizations like the Marine Conservation Society and Rainforest Concern to support conservation* efforts. They ensure that your travel experience is eco-friendly and culturally respectful, while providing top-notch customer service. Specializing in Nordic countries.

BEAT THE CROWDS

Off Season Adventures
http://www.offseasonadventures.com/

Off Season Adventures' mission is to provide remarkable memories while respecting local communities and the environment. Their aim is to encourage off-the-beaten-path immersive experiences during off seasons, steering travelers away from the ordinary, and taking into account the long-term impact of tourism on a destination. They want to empower the traveler to build long lasting and positive relationships with local communities. *As featured in the New York Times, the Good Tourism Blog, Low Season Traveller, Causartist, and the Catalyst.*

Operation Groundswell
www.operationgroundswell.com

Operation Groundswell is an ethical travel company...backpacking with a purpose! Community engagement is at the heart of what they do, crafted by a family of alumni, program leaders, and local partners. They go off-the-beaten-path, from the Himalayas, to the Amazon Jungle, to the shores of the Indian Ocean. *"From peace and justice to quality education and animal conservation, they explore how to make the change we want to see in the world"*. Get involved in community-led initiatives, join farmers in the field, meet activists - roll up your sleeves and get doing.

Pacific Whale Foundation
www.pacificwhale.org

Pacific Whale Foundation is a nonprofit focused on ocean and marine life conservation. They aim to protect the ocean through science and advocacy and inspire environmental stewardship. They run research, education, and conservation programs. Their vision is to protect whales, dolphins, and other marine animals in their natural habitats. *Your ticket to adventure on a PacWhale Eco-Adventures ecotour directly funds nonprofit Pacific Whale Foundation's important work.*

Peruvian Soul
www.peruviansoul.com

Peruvian Soul is about making travel a force for good, benefiting both travelers and locals. They emphasize sustainable tourism by supporting local economies, protecting ecosystems, and preserving cultures. They believe travel fosters empathy and are dedicated to creating positive connections and learning experiences. *Trip Advisor Travelers' Choice Award.*

PURA AVENTURA
www.pura-aventura.com

PURA
AVENTURA
Travel Positive

FORCE FOR GOOD

Pura Aventura started from a chance meeting of its three founders in Chile in the 90s and has grown into a UK travel company certified as a B Corp. Despite changes, their belief in travel as a force for good remains. Since July 2019, they have implemented a significant carbon mitigation plan, using 1% of their revenue for environmental causes. *As featured in Financial Times, National Geographic, The Times, The Telegraph, BBC Radio, and the Guardian.*

Quark Expeditions
www.quarkexpeditions.com

Quark Expeditions is profoundly dedicated to eco-friendly travel, aiming to protect the polar regions they explore. Their *Polar Promise* strategy helps them improve sustainability efforts. Andrew White, the President, emphasizes their commitment to preserving these beautiful areas. *As seen on BBC and Discovery Channel's Frozen Planet.*

Responsible Travel
https://www.responsibletravel.com

"Our holidays are more enjoyable because they do good". Responsible Travel trips are designed to help local communities, protect nature and bring you closer to both. They are one of the world's first responsible holiday companies founded in 2000 and booked over 200,000 customers to date.

Responsible Travel checks all holidays to make sure they are sustainable and responsible and detail their benefits on each page. They also sponsor a day out for a *disadvantaged child* when you travel with them. *As featured in The Guardian, The New York Times, and the Daily Mail.*

Royal Mountain Travel — Nepal

Royal Mountain
www.roalymt.com.np

Royal Mountain Travel, a tour operator in Nepal since 2005, focuses on sustainable tourism by promoting economic empowerment, waste reduction, green tourism, and sustainable communities. They offer a range of tours and expeditions in Nepal, Tibet, and Bhutan. Recognized by international organizations for their commitment to preserving the environment and fostering positive local relationships by *Travelife, TripAdvisor, and Skal International.*

CYCLE THE WORLD

Saddle Skdaddle
www.skedaddle.com

At Skedaddle they love biking around the world, but know it's a privilege and aim to travel responsibly. They try to minimize their impact and give back to the communities you visit. They avoid overtourism by limiting trips and exploring lesser-known places, making for a more enjoyable holiday. Cycling the world for almost 30 years, partners also include *charities like Sustans and Cycling UK.*

Seacology
http://www.seacology.org/

Award-winning Seacology's mission is to protect threatened island ecosystems around the world by working directly with island communities supporting conservation effort from coral reefs, coastal wetlands, mountain forests and most recently mangroves, peatlands, and seagrass. *"Seacology is playing a critically needed role in preserving the vitally important yet very threatened terrestrial and marine ecosystems of islands throughout the world."* – Dr. Sylvia A. Earle, National Geographic Explorer in Residence. Expeditions explore unforgettable islands from coral reefs in Fiji to rainforests in Borneo, and offer you the opportunitie to scuba dive, snorkel, hike, or kayak.

SEVEN**TRAVEL**

Seven Travel
www.seventravel.co.uk

Seven Travel focuses on creating personalized luxury holidays that last ten days or more, allowing you to fully experience a destination...slow travel at its best. They are a luxury travel specialist with a conscience, responsible travel is a core value of their company, and to make sure your unforgettable experience doesn't compromise the very beauty of the place you're visiting. *The Times "top eleven sustainable travel companies going the extra eco-friendly mile", and featured in Forbes, Luxury Travel, Sheelux, The Telegraph, and The Evening Standard.*

SteppesTravel

TREES & SCIENCE

Steppes Travel is committed to promoting positive social and environmental change through travel. *Conde Nast Traveler Top Travel Specialist 2025.* Steppes Travel has supported organizations and projects that focus on conservation like Practical Action, Room to Read, World Land Trust. Steppes also created the forest regeneration scheme *"Trees & Science"* that supports vital research into nuclear fusion, the process that powers the sun that plays a big part in our carbon-free energy future.

OFF THE BEATEN PATH

Undiscovered Mountains
http://www.undiscoveredmountains.com/

Undiscovered Mountains specializes in off the beaten path adventures in the Southern French Alps year round. There Eco-Challenge supports The Conservation Volunteers of the UK, and a carbon offsetting program with Mossy Earth who plants trees on their behalf in a variety of reforestation projects across Europe. They chose the Eco-Challenge as one of their sustainable tourism objectives, to promote winter activities outside of ski resorts and develop a broader tourism economy in surrounding areas. *As seen in The Guardian, BBC Wildlife, Irish Walking Magazine, and Cycling World.*

Up Norway
www.upnorway.com

Up Norway offers unique, customized travel experiences in Norway, focusing on authentic adventures and cultural connections. Be it Viking ancestry, Sami heritage or modern governance they feel proud to share the stories of their small country, consistently placed at the top of the UN Sustainable Development Report as one of the happiest nations in the world. *Non-negotiable commitment that all journeys have a net positive impact on society and nature.*

Wild Sumatra
www.wildsumatra.com

Community-based ecotourism in Indonesia focuses on rainforest and wildlife conservation, as well as local development. They partner with locals to train and support guides, ensuring sustainable, low-impact tours. All funds stay within the local communities, promoting poverty reduction and sustainable growth. *Featured in Lonely Planet and National Geographic Traveler.*

Iceland Unlimited
www.steppestravel.com

Iceland Unlimited is a travel company that offers custom travel packages, including self-drive tours and guided experiences in Iceland, Greenland, and The Faroe Islands. They pride themselves on being the first travel agency in Iceland to specialize in accessible travel. Their team is dedicated to providing stress-free, authentic, and unique holidays, and they have _a five-star rating on TripAdvisor and TripAdvisor's Travelers' Choice Award._

InsideJapan Tours
http://www.insidejapantours.com/

JAPAN FOR ALL

Award-winning Inside Japan is a traditional travel provider but always dreamed of making Japan accessible to all, and this of course extends to travellers with disabilities or mobility issues. They take the guesswork out of a trip to Japan introducing you to the very best sights in Tokyo, Kyoto, Osaka and beyond. _As featured in Time Magazine, Wanderlust, Sunday Mirror, Family Traveller, Daily Telegraph, The Independent, National Geographic, and many more._

Morocco Accessible Travel
http://www.moroccoaccessibletravel.com/

Plan your Moroccan adventure stress-free with accessible tours, adapted camel saddles, mobility equipment rentals, and airport transfers. Whether you seek a luxurious vacation or need a beach wheelchair in Agadir, accessibility solutions are readily available. *Featured in Lonely Planet, Condé Nast Traveller, TripAdvisor, National Geographic, HGTV, and Curb Free with Cory Lee.*

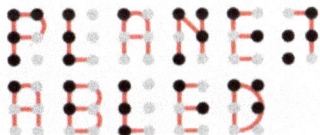

Planet Abled
http://www.planetabled.com/

Award-winning Planet Abled is mainstreaming accessibility and inclusion into the global tourism industry. Planet Abled is on a mission to make the global tourism industry accessible to everyone, with offices in Asia and Europe we work with businesses, travelers, and public service organizations to design inclusive solutions for everyone. Customer centric, inclusive design, technology driven withknowledge sharing. *As seen in The Times of India, Harvard Business Review, The Hindu, Travel+Leisure. Lonely Planet, and Condé Nast Traveller.*

Sage Traveling was founded by John Sage, a wheelchair user who has visited more than 120 cities in Europe. By conducting first-hand accessibility research, John ensures that the advice provided is accurate and reliable regarding hotels, attractions, accommodations, transportation, and itineraries that ensure a smooth trip. *With a global network Sage Traveling accesses the world for all.*

Seaable Holidays
www.seable.co.uk

Award- winning Seable's offers stress-free holidays tailored for the visually impaired community. Just pick a date and destination, and they handle the rest. Their local Seable trained chaperones are *visual aware* to ensure you feel safe and enjoy your trip with activities designed for you and your sighted friends or family. They offer a selection of accessible activities and private excursions that range from sports, food and wine-tasting to sensory experiences suitable for both blind and sighted travellers.

Tapooz Travel
http://www.tapooztravel.com/

Tapooz Travel has grown to become a leading accessible tours and adventures company, with trips across the US and selected global destinations. They have the knowledge, the experience and the resources to tackle even the most complex travel situations. As a matter of fact, Tapooz Travel is one of only a handful of entities *recommended for its accessible travel expertise by Lonely Planet, the world's largest publisher of guide books.*

TRAVELEYES

Traveleyes
www.traveleyes-international.com
in-the-press/

Traveleyes was founded in 2004 by the blind entrepreneur, Amar Latif. They are the world's first commercial tour operator providing independent group travel for people who are blind or partially sighted. Traveleyes' groups are a small and sociable mix of blind and sighted travelers exploring all the senses. As a sighted traveler you can share and describe the world around you, as a blind traveller you have the freedom and independence and you don't have to bring anyone, you'll l join a group of like-minded explorers. Traveleyes' subsidizes the cost of the holiday up to 50%! *As featured in The Guardian, Lonely Planet, The New Zealand Herald, CNN Business Traveller and Wanderlust to name a few.*

Travel for All
Global Accessible Travel Specialists

Travel For All
http://www.travel-for-all.com/

Travel For All is a travel agency that focuses on creating custom vacations for people with disabilities. With over 25 years of experience and connections with over 1,000 suppliers globally, they ensure a hassle-free and enjoyable travel experience. They understand the challenges faced by disabled travelers and provide personalized recommendations and audits to ensure accessibility. Their experts work closely with clients to create confident and stress-free travel itineraries, offering support throughout the entire travel process.

Wheel the World
http://www.wheeltheworld.com/

lvaro Silberstein and Camilo Navarro, lifelong friends, embarked on a dream journey to hike Torres del Paine in Patagonia after Álvaro's car accident left him with a disability. They did it with a special all-terrain wheelchair and shared their story, inspiring many others with disabilities. This led to the creation of Wheel The World, a brand focused on making travel accessible by donating equipment, improving wheelchair accessibility, offering training, and partnering with specialized companies. *Featured in USA Today, BBC, Mashable, Travel Pluse, and Fast Company.*

Book Different
https://www.facebook.com/bookdifferent/about

Award-winning BookDifferent.com is passionate about travel and keeping the planet beautiful. They focus on sustainable and socially responsible travel by offering a hotel booking website where you can find green hotels, and support a charity with every booking. They guarantee the best prices and have a wide selection of hotels, just like other booking sites. Based in the Netherlands.

Community Homestay Network
http://www.communityhomestay.com/

CHN provides an *award-winning* travel experience in Nepal that focuses on creating genuine connections with locals. By immersing travelers in the stories, traditions, and lifestyles of Nepal's people, CHN ensures that every experience is authentic and impactful, going beyond typical sightseeing. *Awards include World Tourism Origination, PATA, Booking.com Booter, IIPT, SDG's Global Startup Competition, and "ones to watch" World Responsible Tourism Award.*

![eco bnb logo]

Ecobnb
www.ecobnb.com

ECO-FRIENDLY BnB

Ecobnb is a community of nearly *two million travelers and 3,000 eco-friendly accommodations across 55 countries.* The Ecobnb focuses on travel experiences that connect with nature, sustainable itineraries, and lesser-known destinations. It promotes responsible travel, slow journeys, and tips to reduce environmental impact, while highlighting accommodations and tour operators investing in sustainability.

ECOHOTELS
www.ecohotels.com

ECO HOTELS

EcoHotels is the booking platform for all eco-certified hotels. Whether you're looking for luxury, budget-friendly, or unique stays, they have something for you. For every hotel booking, they plant a tree. Additionally, they offer you the chance to donate to a sustainability-focused project at no extra cost. To date they have planted 25,000 trees in Denmark at Saltofte Hus and will continue to plant more trees worldwide. Their next tree-planting project will be through the international organization *Tree Nation*.

Fair BnB Coop
http://www.fairbnb.coop.com/

Fair BnB Coop is promoting responsible and sustainable tourism. They help travelers and locals support social and ecological projects in local communities. This community of activists, coders, researchers, and designers focus on making the economy a sharing economy. They offer a people-first alternative that ensures hosts and guests have a great experience, while the community benefits too. This approach is known as Community Powered Tourism. *As seen in The Guardian, Financial Times, Forbes, El Pais, La Repubblica, and Business Insider.*

Farm Stay Planet
www.farmstayplanet.com/

ON THE FARM WORLDWIDE

Farm Stay Planet offers a variety of farm stay accommodations worldwide, from basic B&Bs to luxury farm hotels. The appeal of agritourism lies in reconnecting with our farming heritage and the promise of well-being and benefits to rural areas and communities. They are an affiliate of Booking.com, which deals with most of our reservations on a shared commission basis, and uses a proportion of their revenue to support two important charities: *The One Acre Fund and Farm Forward, a lobby group that fights to reduce animal suffering in the agriculture industry, in particular in the practice of factory farming.*

 **FARMSTAY**

MEET THE FARMERS

Since 2010 Farm Stay USA has been fostering farm stays as a unique immersive travel niche. Passionate about sharing the real stories about the farmers who feed us and their environmental stewardship. Farm Stay USA offers working farms (livestock, crops, flowers, or trees), ranches, vineyards, and animal sanctuaries, to small and large homesteads. Accommodations range from rustic to luxury, tent to inns. You can collect eggs, meet animals, do chores or just take a deep breath and nap. *As seen in Forbes, Mothers, Los Angeles Times, USA Today, and Travel+Leisure.*

AUTHENTIC INDIA

HomeStays of India
www.homestaysofindia.com/about-us/

Award-winning Homestay's goes beyond the expected tourist experience and offers the traveler the opportunity to engage in genuine conversations that deepen understanding of the Indian lifestyle...it gets at the heart and soul of the country through its food, music, dance, vibrant cultural heritage, and authentic way of life. Homestays' portfolio offers modern comforts and conveniences from cities to small villages. Homestays' is dedicated to supporting authentic family run homestays across India that provides local communities with alternate sources of income and helps reduce migration to larger cities.

Rooms For Change
www.roomsforchange.com

RoomsForChange™
Book a Room, Make a Change

Rooms for Change is non-profit that uses their booking platform to find your perfect accommodation - from hotels to home rentals in every style and budget while *giving a Gift of Travel to disadvantaged youth and seniors at no extra cost to you.* Their goal is to grow the community of conscious travelers by providing a more engaging hotel booking platform that helps give back - 100% of their profits go towards creating travel scholarships for disadvantaged youth, seniors and veterans. They're on a mission to enable more people to experience the life-changing power of travel!

Sawday's

Sawday's
www.sawdays.co.uk

Sawday's mission is to bring people together in a way that has a positive social, cultural, and environmental impact. Sawday's is employee owned, has a charitable trust and B Corp certification. Alastair Sawday founded the company over 25 years ago publishing his first book based on notes from his French walking tours, and now has an extensive collection of travel books he's written along with articles for a wide range of publlications.His passion for slow thoughtful travel remains a guiding principle.

Staze is a hotel booking platform for individuals and businesses that enables them to minimize, offset and track a hotel's carbon footprint. By booking through Staze you can offset your carbon footprint for free - they use profits to offset the carbon footprint of every hotel booking. *Committed to achieving Net Zero by 2028, a proud member of the Tech Zero coalition of companies and part of the UNFCC Race to Zero Campaign.*

Earthwatch
http://www.earthwatch.org/

Founded in 1971, renowned Earthwatch connects international volunteers with scientists all over the world in collaborative research critical to understanding and combating climate change, and biodiversity threats. Every year they engage students, teachers, corporate employees, community leaders, and members of the public in research that contributes to innovative environmental solutions. Earthwatch has significantly contributed to conservation by supporting policy plans, protected areas, national parks, and refuges. *"Experience hands-on science in some of the world's most astounding locations. Meet a community of eco-conscious travelers and return home with stories filled with adventure."*

Give
www.givevolunteers.org

Give's *award-winning* trips immerse you in authentic cultural experiences, impactful volunteer work, and unique, off-the-beaten-path adventures - discover the world and uncover your purpose! Locally led and sustainably operated with inclusive 360 support. For one to seven weeks, you'll travel and connect with local cultures, and give back through meaningful volunteer projects. Alongside a community of like-minded travelers, you'll ignite new passions, inspire personal growth, and build lifelong friendships.

VACATIONS WITH PURPOSE

Discovery Corps
https://discovercorps.com/

Discover Corps connects travelers to local communities in a meaningful way. Each trip is designed to impact both the communities and wildlife as well as you or your family, and gives a deeper understanding about the unique and extraordinary parts of the world. Local organizations and leaders bring these experiences to life. Discover Corps seeks partners that are involved in a range of causes and missions that work to improve their communities, local wildlife and world as a whole. *As seen in National Geographic, Los Angeles Times, Afar, Forbes, AARP, and Yoga Digest.*

Grassroots VOLUNTEERING
www.grassrootsvolunteering.org

Grassroots Volunteering is a search engine that connects travelers seeking more purpose in their journey and helps link them to causes and communities that need support. The site lists organizations and small social enterprises around the world along with possible volunteer opportunities. Travelers with weeks and months (years even!) use this search engine to geo-locate community-based organizations in need of your skills or interest.

Venture with Impact
www.venturewithimpact.org

The mission of *Venture with Impact* is to expose professionals to new cultures, people and ideas so they may be more informed and empathetic world citizens, and in the process, provide a positive social impact. Venture with Impact is a 4-week coworking retreat that provides professionals with the opportunity to continue their career remotely (or just take a break from it all) while giving back *through skills-based volunteer projects*. Venture with Impact was founded to end that dilemma and to allow people to work abroad while making a difference where they work and travel - one month at a time!

Fly. Green
www.fly.green

Fly.Green is a unique flight search engine to book your flight and to reduce your climate footprint. The environmental impact of flights is not part of the traditional booking process. Many of us do care about our travels' impact on the environment and many started offsetting their CO_2 footprint in renewable energy projects. So why is online flights search all about "the cheaper the better"? By combining flight search with environmental data and by making offset an integral part of travel, Fly.Green is challenging the traditional ways of travel planning.

EcoTrail International
http://www.ecotrail.com/

EcoTrail® is all about using city trails for various race distances while promoting the importance of protecting nature. They encourage sustainable transport, highlight local heritage, and reduce environmental impact through waste management and eco-friendly practices. The races offer a great way to enjoy trail running and explore cities, emphasizing environmental awareness and cultural heritage.

Eco Trails

Community Tourism And Services

Eco Trails aim is to create a sustainable ecological community by integrating tourism with local economic, cultural, and geographical attractions. Through activities like treks, forest yoga, and village life experiences, they seek to raise awareness, empower local communities, foster economic development, and contribute to natural conservation. The initiative promotes knowledge sharing between travelers and locals, benefiting both parties economically and culturally.

GuruWalk
www.guruwalk.com

Award-winning GuruWalk is a huge global community for free walking tours, connecting travelers with guides in over 800 cities across 100 countries. Their goal is to make culture accessible and create a more empathetic society through unique and quality experiences. They pride themselves on being more than just a platform, considering themselves a family.

S&K
RECOMMENDED
BLOGS & PODCASTS

S&K RECOMMENED BLOGS & PODCASTS

PLEASE NOTE: Some bloggers and podcasters have several outlets like newsletters, websites, YouTube shows, and a few have both a podcast and blog. The listings have been divided into bloggers and podcasters (even if they have both) to give you as many voices as possible.

As with the other curated recommendations in the book, there are some amazing bloggers and podcasters out there focused on travel - many are funny, charming, engaging and inspirational, but for the purpose of the directory the selections were based on the criteria previously mentioned: sustainability as a key principle, readers/listener reviews, overall ratings and feedback within the community of responsible travelers and travel professionals.

CONSIDER: There are travel bloggers and podcasters offering a wide range of discussions that address the finances of travel, living the nomad life, logistics, being a retired nomad, LGBTQ travel, traveling with disabilities, and luxury travel. Please enjoy these opinions, recommendations and engaging conversations through the lens of a responsible and sustainable traveler... adventure on!

JOHN TORRES -
AGAINST THE COMPASS
http://againststhecompass.com/

The goal of *Against The Compass* is to encourage travelers to explore off-the-beaten track, often misunderstood, destinations from Pakistan to Iraq, Syria, Yemen, Saudi Arabia and more. John is from Barcelona, Spain and quit his corporate job to start traveling to help break the stereotypes about these countries, and inspire others to do the same. He offers group expeditions every month that explores the people and culture of these unique unexpected destinations. *Featured in Lonely Planet, The Guardian, Washington Post, Sky News, France 24, El Pais and more.*

BIANCA CARUANA -
ALTRUISTIC TRAVELLER
https://theartruistictraveller.com/

Award-winning The Altruistic Traveller has evolved from just a blog to curating content that focuses on stories, news and insights about sustainable tourism and it's challenges. The platform exists to share, advocate and discuss how to travel with more integrity and compassion. In 2023 Bianca published her memoir Soul Truth, a journey from corporate success to *"...a story of love, loss, community, and connection, infused with sage wisdom about the journey to meet our untethered selves for the first time."*

FORUM & SHIVA -
BARRIERS & BOARDERS
https://barriersandboarders.com/

Born and raised in India, Forum and Shiva inspire eco-conscious travel that explores worlds beyond your own boarders. They are both architects passionate about building with natural materials using regional practices, and have a deep love for nature and vegan food. Join their "cozy corner" and read stories about local communities, off-the-beaten-path destinations and what they've learned along the way.

BECKI ENRIGHT -
BORDERS OF ADVENTURE
http://www.bordersofadventure.com/

Becki is an *award-winning* writer, author and adventurous explorer. Her blog is about responsible travel and changing perceptions and narratives about misunderstood countries or regions in the context of their history, politics, and culture. *"... how I set to inform and encourage others – to travel differently, adventurously, responsibly and with purpose."* She has appeared on *Sky News and CNN discussing North Korea, and been features in Lonely Planet, National Geographic, Wanderlust, New York Times, Time, Grazia, The Guardian, Buzzfeed and more.*

CHARLIE MERCHANT & LUKE NICHOLSON - CHARLIE ON TRAVEL
http://www.charlieontravel.com/

CHARLIE ON TRAVEL

Charlie and Luke are digital nomads and bloggers based in the UK. They are storytellers, photographers, influencers, and responsible travelers who want to inspire and encourage others to travel responsibly. "Named as top *UK travel bloggers, Charlie on Travel* is trusted by thousands to plan their travel adventures and learn about responsible travel." They work on campaigns for tourism boards, travel companies, hotels, restaurants and travel gear brands. *Featured on BBC Radio, Five News, HuffPost, Skyscanner, and Marie Claire.* .

OKSANA & MAX - DRINK TEA & TRAVEL
https://drinkteatravel.com/

Drink Tea & Travel is an *award-winning* beautiful sustainable travel blog. Canadians Oksana and Max's mission is to inspire an unconventional way of living, sustainable travel practices, and how to make a positive impact on the destinations and communities you visit. They've summited Mt.Kilimanjaro, drank tea with Bedouins, and slept under the stars in Mongolia...join them on their next adventure!

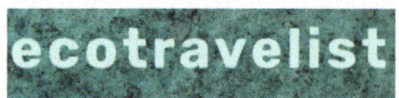

SARAH REID - ECOTRAVELIST
http://www.ecotravelist.com/

As an *award-winning* writer Sarah developed an understanding of the impact tourism has on the planet and people. Disturbed by the lack of awareness and misinformation surrounding sustainable tourism, she established ecotravelist to help travelers plan trips responsibly. She has a Graduate Certificate in Sustainable Tourism Management, and written two books for Lonely Planet *(The Sustainable Travel Handbook and Sustainable Escapes)*. Her awards include *Travel Writer of the Year* by the Australian Society of Travel Writers, and *Specialist Travel Writer of the Year*: emerging Destinations at the *UK's Travel Media Awards.*.

WILDLIFE & SANCTUARIES

KETKI GADRE- EXPLORE WITH ECOKATS
https://explorewithecokats.com/

Ketki is from India and has been writing and documenting her travels since 2017. From 22 states in India to 15 countries, her main focus has been on wildlife sanctuaries and national parks, with a "dash" of other sites with a sustainability focus. Ketki teaches environmental ecosystems at the university, helps NGOs with environmental publications, and contributes to in-flight magazines and publications in India. *Featured in Travel Escapades, NAMASTE.ai, Spice Route, and Deccan Herald.*.

STEFANIA GUGLIELMI - EVERY STEPH
http://www.everysteph.com/

EVERY STEPH
Green & Glamorous Travel and Lifestyle

Stefania is from the beautiful city of Bologna, her motto "green is the new black"! In her blog she redefines what the stereotypical eco-traveler might be...yes a little glam and luxury can go hand in hand with being a responsible traveler. With a Bachelor's Degree in International Studies, a Master's in Communications and Digital Marketing, Stefania decided to take the road less traveled to freedom, and being a full-time blogger. *As seen in Business Insider, Refinery 29, DO Something.org, Tripadvisor, and Yahoo Money.*

GirlabouttheGlobe

LISA IMOGE ELDRID - GIRLS ABOUT THE GLOBE
https://www.girlabouttheglobe.com/

The *award-winning Girl About The Globe,* is a blog for socially conscious women traveling solo. Lisa has travelled to 147 countries (115 solo), her aim is to empower women to make a difference and promote sustainable travel. *Her goal, create 100,000 socially conscious travellers that will impact 100,000 vulnerable girls by 2030...*book through her site to help achieve that goal! Partnered with War Child, The Code, Sustainable Travel International, and Travel Aware. *Featured in BBC Radio, New York Times, USA Today, Skyscanner, and Wanderlust Travel Magazine.*

GREEN GLOBAL TRAVEL

BRET LOVE & MARY GABBERT-GREEN GLOBAL TRAVEL
http://greenglobaltravel.com/

With over 300,000 followers, Green Global Travel has been a passionate leader in encouraging (and educating) travelers to embrace sustainable travel, and what that means, from environmental conservation and cultural preservation, to protecting wildlife. *"Ecotourism is an adventure that changes lives."* In their blog they try to strike a balance between raising awareness through informative articles to keeping the reader engaged and encouraged. *Featured in BBC, USA Today, NPR, National Geographic, World Wildlife Fund, Lonely Planet and more.* .

ANNA & ANTHONY - GREEN MOCHILA
https://greenmochila.com/

Green Mochila
Budget Backpacking in South America

The idea to write the Green Mochila travel blog was inspired by their love curiosity about the people of South America, their beliefs, hopes, dreams and the history of their country. As eco-mindset travellers, Anna and Anthony are focused on budget backpacking in South America, they offer travel tips, city & country guides, and recommend itineraries. They encourage the "lesser-known path" sustainably and with more pleasure. Their guides are designed for slow travel, no planes, less plastic and wandering at your own pace without tours.

STEFANY SEIPP-
GREEN PEARLS
http://www.greenpearls.com/

GREEN PEARLS®
UNIQUE PLACES

Green Pearls ® focuses on travel, architecture, food and sustainable lifestyles. It's about having fun while being environmentally aware and making the right choices along the way. They offer green lifestyle tips for sourcing ethical fashion, finding sustainable architecture, green destinations, eco hotels to recipes and birdwatching. *"Green Pearls® is a leading source for green hotels around the world. We chose our members based on their sustainable initiatives and their green projects. The Green Pearls® requirements need to be fulfilled by every member by at least 80%.*

A COLLECTIVE -
GREEN SUITCASE TRAVEL
http://www.greensuitcasetravel.com/

"We are a collection of influencers and innovators with a background in a variety of converging industries. We came together as artists, thinkers, and like-minded individuals with a passion to redefine the way we travel. To travel on purpose." Green Suitcase not only shares their experience through their blog, but helps you plan and customize your sustainable trip from packing tips to flights, getting around, accommodations, what to do (e.g. culture events or volunteering), and after the trip recaps your carbon footprint.

COMMUNITY-
GOOD TOURISM (GT)
http://www.goodtourismblog.com/

"Dedicated to a truly sustainable and sincerely responsible travel & tourism industry; featuring news, opinions, stories, and evolving best practices". Good Tourism's insights are posts from experts, practitioners, and academics who want to share their sustainable tourism in plain English for travelers' who want to dig deeper, and general tourism stakeholders. Good Tourism is connecting the dots between theory, practice, opinions, and best practices. Good Tourism's Destinations & Places is about confident destinations, special places and tourism stakeholders who want to highlight their programs and actions that support sustainable tourism.

ANNA CHAHUNEAU -
GREEN WANDERLUST
https://greenwanderlust.org/

GREEN WANDERLUST

With over *3 million subscribers on YouTube,* French world traveller Anna has created a unique blog that is more than a blog - through her photographer, storytelling and videography she creates a remarkable journey into the beauty she seeks in the vast landscapes of nature and human experience. She has a degree in Biology and Chinese and created the prized documentary *Pursuing The Monarchs.* With her blog she shares her tips, travel itineraries and benefits of slow travel. *"...my love for traveling runs deep, so does my love for our planet and as a concerned scientist and earth advocate, I make a point of traveling and living as sustainably as I can"*

JUSTIN CEKSTERS & LAUREN YAKIWCHUK- JUSTIN + LAUREN
https://justinpluslauren.com/

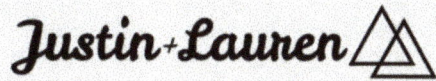

Award-winning full-time blogger and photographer, Lauren, is the content creator - from sustainable travel, wellness travel, vegan travel, outdoor adventures to city explorations. Justin produces beautiful cinematic and vlog-style videos. With over 100,000 monthly views, Justin and Lauren also highlight coffee shops, cafes and craft beer destinations along with bucket list adventures and off-beat discoveries. *As seen on Lonely Plant, BBC Earth, Business Insider, CBC, and Toronto Star Explore.*

PASSPORT STAMP COLLECTOR

LOLA MÉNDEZ - MISS FILATELISTA
http://www.missfilatelista.com/

Lola is a Uruguayan American freelance journalist, her articles on travel have been published in *Lonely Planet, CNN, Matador Network and Atlas Obscura, as well as essays for Oprah, InStyle, Cosmopolitan and Huffington Post.* She is dedicated to sustainable travel, seeking out ethical experiences that benefit local communities, and trades flying for buses, taxis, boats and horses - "y'know climate change is a kind of thing". She has also appeared in *Fast Company, Thrillist, Condé Nast Traveler and Travel Latina.*

ERIK GAUGER- NOTES FROM THE ROAD
http://www.notesfromtheroad.com/

Notes from the Road is an "unvarnished, messy and truthful look at travel from a regular guy". Started in 1999, Notes from the Road is one of the longest-running blogs on the internet. Staying independent and true to his original vision, Erik's writing and photography has always focused on people, ideas, and faraway places. He considers travel blogging a powerful medium in addressing activist issues, and the impact of tourism on the environment and local communities. Featured in Condé Nast Traveler.

EXPERIMENTAL & UNVARNISHED

Jim O'Donnell Photography

PASSIONATE PHOTOGRAPHER

JIM O'DONNELL -
JIM O'DONNELL PHOTOGRAPHY
http://www.aroundtheworldineightyyears.com/

Jim is an archeologist, journalist, author, lecturer, explorer, and conservation photographer with a passionate connection to landscapes, wildlife, and people. His writing covers topics like climate change, tourism, and environmental conservation. He is also working on a novel and a non-fiction travel book. Based in Taos, New Mexico, Jim's work spans wildlife, agricultural, and urban landscapes globally. *His work has appeared in several publications like National Geographic Maps, BBC, Destinations and Taos Magazine.* " I create powerful visual stories in order to positively impact the lives of people around the world."

PAULINA WEIS - PAULINA ON THE ROAD
https://paulinaontheroad.com/

SLOW TRAVELER

The multi *award-winning Paulina on the Road* blog, is about slow sustainable travel like hiking, sailing and cycling. She encourages slow travel and getting back to the roots of what travel used to mean, connecting with people, cultures and nature. Paulina has a master's degree in Intercultural Communications and European Studies with a special interest in linguistics and language, qualities that give her unique insights and perspectives as a multicultural blogger. *As featured in LA Weekly, Voyage New York, FLUX Magazine, and European Business Magazine.*

ERIN HYNES - PINA TRAVEL
https://pinatravels.org/

CURIOUS TRAVELER

Erin is the creator of the *award-winning Pina Travels* and host of *Curious Tourism* (listed previously). Her blog and guides cover responsible travel, from how to avoid overtourism, to tips on how to travel sustainably. She was shortlisted for an award for "Best Responsible Piece," Traverse Creator Awards 2024, won Best Written Piece in 2022, and featured in *Business Insider, AFAR Media, Toronto Star, and True North Living.* She has also appeared on various podcasts from *iHeart Radio to The Thoughtful Travel podcast and CBC's Podcast Playlist.*

COMMUNITY- POSTCARD TRAVEL CLUB
http://www.postcard.travel/

Postcard Travel Club was established to bring together a global community of conscientious luxury travelers, boutique properties, travel designers, and destination experts who share a vision for responsible tourism. It enables members to collect unique postcards, share travel inspiration, and connect directly with trusted, invitation-only partners and thereby contribute to a more conscious and sustainable future for luxury travel. *"Join us and be part of a movement that is redefining the way we explore the world and making travel a force for good. Postcard partners are a value-aligned collective that brings together brands that advance responsible tourism.*

SPECK ON THE GLOBE

JABBIE SYNAM - SPECK ON THE GLOBE
https://speckontheglobe.com/

JAbbie is a writer and journalist - traveling and sharing ethical and responsible tourism stories in over 100 countries since 2013. She is the resident sustainable tourism expert for Wander Community (a global travel collective) and judge for Marie Claire's Sustainability Awards in 2023. *She has been featured in Business Insider, The Globe, The Culture Trip, Rewire, Matador Network, USA Today, Inside Himalayas, and more.* She continues her travels looking for "eco-friendly accommodations, wildlife conservation efforts, and ways to be a better traveler".

LUCIE -
THE MINDFUL TRAVELLER
http://www.exploremindfully.com/

THE MINDFUL TRAVELLER
SLOW EXPLORATION

Lucie, born in France and now living in the UK, decided years ago to change her path from becoming a lawyer to following her passion of photography, writing, exploring the world, and sharing her art to inspire others. Through her travels she became bothered by the negative behaviors and disregard for nature and communities of many tourists which lead to a Master's Degree based on her memoir about social media and the impact of travel - it shaped her future work around sustainable and responsible travel - *"be a traveller not a tourist"*.

@thepoortraveler

YOSH DIMEN & VINS CARLOS - THE POOR TRAVELER
https://thepoortraveler.net/

The *award-wining The Poor Traveler* is a blog that caters to casual travelers who are budget-conscious but willing to spend on valuable experiences. Their focus is on ethical and sustainable practices, from your carbon footprint, to the impact of tourism on local communities. Their aim is to provide free travel guides based on their experiences and lessons learned, especially for those new to traveling. The term "poor" in the blog's name refers to being unfortunate or unlucky, reflecting the authors' early travel mistakes and financial struggles. *Awarded USA #1 Budget Travel Blog and Best Travel Blog in Asia and also featured in BBC, Time, CNN, The Huffington Post, Buzzfeed and more.*

The Shooting Star
SLOW, SOULFUL, SUSTAINABLE TRAVEL

SHIVYA NATH-
THE SHOOTING STAR
http://the-shooting-star.com/blog/

Shivya, the creator of the award-winning sustainable travel blog *Shooting Star*, is a writer, photographer, storyteller, nomad, social entrepreneur, vegan, environmentalist, and slow traveler. Her writings sit at the intersection of travel, environment conservation, and the well-being of communities. She grew up at the base of the Himalayan Mountains in India wondering, as a child, "...what lay beyond the mountains I could see from my rooftop". *Featured on BBC, National Geographic (cover), Washington Post, Travel + Leisure, and named one of thirty Global Champions at the Global Hospitality Awards in 2022.*

NICOLE MELANCON-
THIRDEYEMOM
https://thirdeyemom.com/

Thirdeyemom
Traveling the World and Doing Good

Nicole is a highly recognized freelance journalist, blogger and advocate for good. She has been published in *National Geographic, BBC, Toronto Star, and she is the Content Editor for GLP Films*. Over the last 15 years her blog has focused on sustainable travel, solo and family travel in combination with topics like global health, human rights, women and girls' empowerment, food insecurity and environmental conservation. Nicole has also been a voice and advocate for Save the Children, WaterAid, UNICEF, Doctors without Borders, Solar Sister, the United Nations Foundation, Too Young to Wed and the ONE Campaign.

CRISTINA GARCIA & HAL BRINDLEY - TRAVEL FOR WILDLIFE
http://www.travel4wildlife.com/

Award-winning Travel For Wildlife was founded by zoologist Cristina and wildlife photographer Hal. Their mission is to support and promote responsible wildlife tourism highlighting adventures around the world. Cristina, born and raised in Barcelona, is on the Board of Directors of SEE Turtles, a non-profit sea turtle conservation organization. Hal has a master's in conservation Biology, his photography has appeared in magazines like *Asia Geographic and TV shows like National Geographic "Caught In the Act"*. They also founded Truly Wild an eco-conscious clothing company dedicated to wildlife conservation.

KATHRYN BURRINGTON - TRAVEL WITH KAT
https://thepoortraveler.net/

Award-winning Travel With Kat is her personal blog started in 2011, where she shares her passion for discovering new countries, cultures and cuisines. Kat's photography has appeared in many national and international publications including *Lonely Planet, The Independent on Sunday, Hello, and Marie Claire.* She is passionate about animals and human rights, and sustainable travel. She is an active supporter of *PLAN International, Action Aid, Amnesty International and Fairtrade Foundation and qualified as a responsible whale watching guide by the World Cetacean Alliance.*

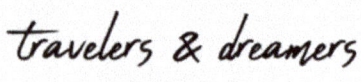

**ANNELIES-
TRAVELERS AND DREAMERS**
https://travelersanddreamers.com/

The Travelers & Dreamers blog is about mindful travel with a mission to inspire plant based food and slow sustainable travel practices. Her goal is to help the reader make sustainable choices that protects the environment and wildlife, supports local communities, and makes your journey authentic and meaningful. *Featured in U.S. News and World Reports, The New Zealand Herald, allBusiness, Be Vegan, and Parade.*

TRAVE LIKE IT MATTERS

*EMILY & AARON -
TWO DUSTY TRAVELERS
https://twodustytravelers.com/*

Emily is journalist and registered nurse *dedicated to humanitarian nursing and has volunteered in numerous countries like an Ebola clinic in West Africa.* Aaron is a teacher, photographer, technology expert, and Eagle Scout. They advocate for ethical and sustainable travel, emphasizing the impact of travel choices on destinations. They aim to inspire meaningful travel that broadens understanding of humanity and positively impacts visited places. Read Emily's postings on Substack for updates. Substack and Facebook, a place to foster a community of caring and curious people interested in making the world a little better

ERIN HYNES & KATTIE LAUR - CURIOUS TOURISM
Available on: Apple Podcasts and Spotify

Award-winning Curious Tourism is a monthly Canadian podcast that explores the true nature of what it means to be a responsible traveler, and sustainable tourism in general. Erin and Kattie interview guests on a wide range of topics from dark tourism to volunteerism and privileged travel. *Featured in Apple's New & Noteworthy, Toronto Star, CBC's Podcast Playlist and shortlisted for several awards. And, hit the podcast charts in Canada, USA, Ireland, UK and Places & Travel.*

JEFF GREENWALD - ETHICAL TRAVELER
Available on: Apple iTunes

The *Ethical Traveler* podcast, hosted by Jeff Greenwald, aims to highlight the *transformative power of travel through interviews with various personalities, global music, news, and contests.* It offers travel tips, showcases environmental efforts, and encourages community involvement. Travel is a significant global industry, impacting nearly one in ten people. Jeff Greenwald, the executive director of Ethical Traveler and an accomplished author, brings a wealth of experience, including work in Cambodian refugee camps and creating the first international travel blog.

DEBBIE CLARKE & JOSIE MAJOR-GOOD AWAITS
Available on: Apple Podcasts, Spotify, Amazon Music, iHeart Radio.

GOOD *Awaits* podcast is a part of The Center for GOOD Travel, a social enterprise (www.good-travel.org) based in New Zealand. Debbie and Josie's podcast is a community-based platform for travellers, students, academics and tourism leaders to listen, discuss and discover what the future might be locally...and globally. It is a journey into how to reimagine tourism in New Zealand and what it might mean to be truly regenerative, one that nurtures the wellbeing of communities and ecosystems as it is being threatened by the climate crises.

RISE INSTITUTE - RISE PODCAST
Available on: Apple Podcasts, Podbean, Spotify, Amazon Music, and iHeart Radio

Award-winning RISE Travel Institute is committed to empowering travelers and travel professionals through education. The RISE podcast brings together scholars, activities, travelers and tourism professionals to discuss and think deeply about how travel can uplift communities, protect natural resources and bring travel to a more responsible and ethical experience.

CHRISTINE WINEBRENNER - SOUL OF TRAVEL PODCAST
Available on: Apple Podcasts, Spotify, and YouTube

The *award-winning Soul of Travel Podcast*, is about mindful impact driven travel. You will hear stories and wisdom from celebrated women who are making a difference in how and why we travel, from beyond-the-bucket list, to intentional purpose driven travel that empowers the audience to be a compassionate traveler. *"It explores transformational travel that supports gender equity, turning travelers into agents of change. Recognized for fostering an inclusive space, Soul of Travel advocates for equitable, meaningful travel experiences that create deep connections."*

AMANDA KENDLE - THE THOUGHTFUL TRAVEL PODCAST
Available on: Apple Podcasts, Spotify, IHeart Radio, Listen Notes, Omny.fm, and TuneIn.

Amanda's podcast has been a favorite of travel lovers since 2016. A travel addict herself from Perth, Amanda hosts a show where guests share their experiences, from the people they've met, what they learned along the way, and those memorable meals. More practical subjects range from the use of a foreign language, overtourism, getting lost, interacting with animals, travel trends and even resolutions.

JAMES HAMMOND-
WINGING IT TRAVEL PODCAST
Available on: Apple Podcasts, Spotify,
IHeart Radio, Listen Notes,
Amazon Music.

Winging It Travel Podcast is a laid-back podcast dedicated to exploring the world from adventure to cultural immersions and making those important connections. James shares his own experiences and has conversations with world's most diverse and well-travelled people. *"With a knack for finding hidden gems and sharing travel hacks, James inspires listeners to embrace spontaneity and push beyond their comfort zones."*

JASON MOORE - ZERO TO TRAVEL
PODCAST (and blog)
Available on: Apple Podcasts,
Spotify, IHeart Radio, Amazon Music,

With *12 million downloads, 195 countries and over 800 5-star reviews,* the *Zero To Travel Podcast* will give you life-changing perspectives that will inspire along with practical advice from finances to logistics. *Featured in The Washington Post, Outside, Forbes, Travel + Leisure, and The Telegraph.*

S&K
RECOMMENDED
MAGAZINES

S&K RECOMMENED RECOMMENED MAGAZINES
(DIGITAL & PRINT)

PLEASE NOTE: As with the previous sections of the directory, magazines (digital and print) have additional outlets and channels like apps, blogs, podcasts, videos, films, newsletters, guides, and books. Most of the "magazines" are more like websites, it can get a bit fuzzy in defining them one way or the other unless they specify as a digital magazine or have a print version.

The majority of magazines being recommended are award-winning and visually stunning,with writing and storytelling that will inspire curiosity and hopefully your next journey...or how you want to live your life as a nomad! There are two sections of listings, the main section features magazines focused on sustainable travel specifically, the second listings are eco-friendly lifestyle magazines that also include sections and articles on sustainable travel. The latter was important to include because of their overall focus on sustainable living that includes travel in the overall picture.

CONSIDER: When visiting some of your favorite fashion and lifestyle websites and magazines you will find most have features on eco-friendly buying, or environmental note articles on travel that might include gear.

AFAR
http://www.afar.com/

Award-winning AFAR is a beautiful purpose-driven media brand that believes that the power of travel can make the world a better place through experiences that enrich the traveler, support local communities and protect natural resources. Their audience is a community of conscientious global travelers who "arrive in a new place with humility and desire to learn from others". *The AFAR Travel Advisory Council,* made up of travel professionals across the country, are available to help you plan your next trip.

Atlas Obscura
http://www.atlasobscura.com/

"Adventures driven by curiosity." Widely celebrated *Atlas Obscura's* mission is to inspire wonder and curiosity about our remarkable world. "We are a publisher of best-in-class journalism about hidden places, incredible history, scientific marvels, and gastronomical wonders." Their first book, Atlas Obscura: *An Explorer's Guide to the World's Hidden Wonders hit number one on the bestsellers list of the New York Times.* Atlas Obscura Adventures' designs trips to do good, they consider carefully the impact on communities, ecosystems, and the planet. They've partnered with Intrepid (largest travel B-Corp) to ensure their trips are sustainable and responsible.

Condé Nast Traveler

Condé Nast Travel International
https://barriersandboarders.com/

DIGITAL / PRINT / PODCAST NEWSLETTER / VIDEO

Highly regarded award-winning *Condé Nast Traveler* has been a leading voice in travel since 1987, providing inspiration and up-to-date discerning information. They emphasizes the importance of not wasting time during travel by leveraging a network of experts and contributors. The Global Advisory Board, composed of industry experts from various sectors worldwide, guides the brand on critical travel issues. *Editor Thani highlights the magazine's focus on sustainability, inclusivity, transformation, and authentic local experiences.*

Flightless Travel
http://www.flightlesstravel.com/

DIGITAL / TRIP PLANNING

In an era where speed is the name of the game, slow travel offers a refreshing alternative, allowing travelers to savor experiences and connect with diverse people and wildlife. The founders, Tom and Lorraine McMillan, created the website to advocate for surface travel inspired by their journey from Singapore to Scotland in 2008, involving numerous buses, trains, boats, and tuk tuks over 85 days! Surface travel emphasizes the significance of the journey itself, highlighting memorable destinations and interactions, proving that traditional travel can surpass air travel in creating lasting memories. *Featured The Sunday Times, The Observer, BBC and more.*

Epicure & Culture Magazine
https://epicureandculture.com

Epicure&Culture
FOOD, WINE & CULTURE FOR THE ETHICAL TRAVELER

Epicure & Culture, founded by Jessie Festa in 2012, aims to inspire meaningful and responsible travel by emphasizing sustainable tourism, immersive cultural experiences, and local food and drink stories. Jessie also manages the solo female travel blog *Jessie on a Journey and NYC Photo Journeys*. Her work has been featured in notable publications such as *USA Today, CNN, Business Insider, Thrillist, and WestJet Magazine*. The magazine guides travelers on how to thoughtfully engage with the world, offering insights into local cuisines, traditions, and cultures.

travel through a
local lens

Global Yodal
http://www.globalyodel.com/

Global Yodel is a worldwide community that facilitates and encourages cultural exchange through creativity, arts, and travel. It connects people by allowing them to share life and culture from a local's perspective. The magazine/website promotes the work of photographers, filmmakers, artists, and designers, offering insights into various locations from those who know them best. Conceived from a passion for exploration, *Global Yodel* serves as an interactive forum to showcase global lifestyles, special places, and events.

GlobeRovers
https://globerovers.com/

GlobeRovers was created in Hong Kong in 1997 during the handover of Hong Kong to China. Roving the Globe, intrepidly, *GlobeRovers* follows the off-the-beaten-track route to bring you destinations you may know little about. "GlobeRovers travels so you can see the world." *GlobeRovers* Magazine is a published twice a year (July and December) and is available in digital and printed formats. Website features photo essays, destinations, maps, and visual explorations. *GlobeRovers* focuses on bringing exciting destinations and inspiring photography from around the globe to the intrepid traveller.

Go Nomad
http://www.gonomad.com/

DIGITAL / PRINT / BLOG
BOOKS

Top ranked twenty-year-old GoNOMAD Travel is an alternative travel portal offering fresh travel articles, accurate destination guides, and listings of tour companies, along with options for booking air, rail, hotels, and cars. Editor Max Hartshorne provides extensive coverage of destinations through articles, podcasts, radio shows, and social media. They offer a broad range of travel options including alternative travel and volunteering opportunities as well. GoNOMAD is ranked among the top five travel websites globally and has been a media sponsor for major travel shows like the NY Times Travel Show and WTM.

GOMad Nomad
https://gomadnomad.com/

"World Travel Food Culture for Independent Travelers" Founder and Editor, Stephen Bugno, was inspired to create the concept of GoMad Nomad based on his decades of travel, work, and volunteering in over 100 countries. With a community of over 25,000 travelers, the on-line magazine caters to the independent traveler interested in food, culture, off-the-beaten-track destinations, volunteering, budget and alternative travel. The Travel Desk section of the magazine offers unique perspectives with shared stories and "cultural snippets"

greentraveller.co.uk
Est. 2006

Green Traveller Magazine
https://greentraveller.co.uk/

The Green Traveller magazine includes feature stories, flight-free routing in Europe, a newsletter and over 50 green travel eGuides. Contributors to the eGuides are made up of a community of travel writers, photographers, videographers and bloggers. The focus of the eGuides is on low-impact travel, protecting the livelihoods of local communities, conservation of the environment and natural habitats. The holiday recommendations include local food & drink, where to stay, and low-impact visits like gardens, observing wildlife, or museums. The blog addresses the questions surrounding the challenges of travel during what is"a climate and nature emergency

In The Know Traveler
https://intheknowtraveler.com/

Devin Galaudet, Editor and Publisher of *In The Know Traveler (ITKT)*, has written for the *Huffington Post, Technorati, The Citron Review,* and the *Two Hawks Quarterly literary journal*. The on-line magazine is *dedicated to cultural exchange through travel*...needed now more than ever! His stories, videos, and photos cover 189 countries driven by the desire to get more Americans traveling internationally and realizing how much we all have in common as human beings - and in the end foster understanding that can reduce conflict. ITKT has been around since 2004 featuring writers from around the world and is proud of being a non-corporate entity.

Matador Network
https://matadornetwork.com/

The *award-winning and stunning Matador* envisions travel as transformative, a force for good with the power to connect and find our humanity in each other. Their mission is to inspire a new and diverse generation of travelers to be "fearless" though their stores, videos and films. Matador's "Global Citizen" immersive video series challenges stereotype and inspires responsible travel that embraces the beauty and fragility of our planet. Narratives for the magazine and videos are drawn from a community of travel influencers who uncover remarkable stores, hidden gems, diverse cultures, wildlife, nature, and reveal "the human experience."

Outlook Travel Magazine
http://www.outlooktraveller.com/

India's mostly widely read travel magazines and website, Outlook Traveller, is dedicated to bringing the reader honest, unique, and authentic insights about a broad range of destinations with stunning photographs and a reader-friendly journalistic approach to storytelling. The Outlook Responsible Tourism Initiative brings issue-based stories about protecting and preserving India's heritage, from monuments to art, endangered wildlife to musical traditions. Featured experiences range from heritage, food, adventure, spiritual and more.

Perceptive Travel
http://www.perceptivetravel.com/

Established in 2006, the highly awarded *Perceptive Travel* is an online travel magazine featuring award-winning authors and considered the "best travel writing" anthology of writers from around the world digging deep with unique and authentic perspectives. Perceptive Travel's has won awards from *"Society of American Travel Writers, the North American Travel Journalists Association, the Solas Awards, the Travel Media Association of Canada Awards, and the Northern Lights Awards. Our opt-in newsletter list is a who's who of book publishing acquisition editors, travel magazine editors, and publicists."* The Editor, Time Leffel, has been a keynote speaker and panelist at various industry events and is frequently quoted in major media outlets.

ROADS & KINGDOMS

Roads & Kingdoms
https://intheknowtraveler.com/

The stunning and highly awarded *Roads & Kingdoms* is based on a simple idea, food can be the "window into our humanity". *R&K has won Primetime Emmy's partnering with Anthony Bourdain, won National Magazine Awards, and named James Beard Publication of the Year in 2017.* Their latest evolution, The League of Travelers, is small group culinary travel lead by chefs, writers, and raconteurs, it brings people together through remarkable food in extraordinary destinations. In collaboration with chef Jose Andrés and the estate of the late and great partner Anthony Bourdain, created a once in a lifetime experience. Five percent of net proceeds benefits *World Central Kitchen.*

Wanderlust
https://matadornetwork.com/

Since 1993 the *award-winning* beautiful *Wanderlust* magazine is the leading UK travel magazine committed to responsible, conscious and sustainable travel. Wanderlust's stunning photography and editorials cover immersive authentic travel experiences, from off-the-beaten-path to off-season destinations, wildlife and adventure travel, cultural heritage travel with additional new coverage on history, archology and urban destinations. In 2023 Wanderlust lunched the Travel Green List, an annual list of inspiring and sustainable travel.

Green Living
https://greenlivingmag.com/

Green Living Magazines is a lifestyle magazine with a mission to educate, inspire and empower readers to make the right choices for a healthy planet and life '...to live, work, and play sustainably leaving the world a better place for future generations' The magazine features a wide range of resources from travel, fashion, home, design and technology, to health and wellness...a daily lifestyle centered on living green.

National Geographic
http://www.nationalgeographic.com/

Hard to know what to say about the world renowned and highly awarded *National Geographic,* it's been part of our lives since 1888, but it would be neglect not to include this remarkable national treasure. They have extensive articles about sustainable tourism and their *National Geographic Center for Sustainable Destinations* has been moved forward through the *Destination Stewardship Center* - they provide information about the protection and stewardship of destinations. When you travel with *National Geographic Society* it helps support grants to storytellers, educators, innovators and scientists around the world.

DIGITAL/EVENTS WORKSHOPS / VIRTUAL FESTIVALS

Pebbles' is an eco-friendly guide to a stylish sustainable lifestyle, they inform and inspire a more ethical approach to living - waste less, lower your carbon footprint...use less plastic! They feature stories and resources on sustainable travel, style, low waste living, home, ethical fashion, business, food and more. Their travel section focuses on slow mindful journeys using trains and bikes instead of planes, connecting with locals in a meaningful way, and appreciating other cultures with an open mind. *It's a magazine about moving towards a future where the terms eco and ethical are just the way we live.* Featured in Forbes.

DIGITAL / PRINT / TV VIDEO / SHOP

Sublime
http://sublimemagazine.com/

Since 1993 the *award-winning* beautiful *Wanderlust* magazine is the leading UK travel magazine committed to responsible, conscious and sustainable travel. Wanderlust's stunning photography and editorials cover immersive authentic travel experiences, from off-the-beaten-path to off-season destinations, wildlife and adventure travel, cultural heritage travel with additional new coverage on history, archology and urban destinations. In 2023 Wanderlust lunched the Travel Green List, an annual list of inspiring and sustainable travel.

Treehugger
http://www.treehugger.com/

Treehugger
Sustainability for All.

For over twenty-years Treehugger has been offering clarity and inspiration on green living driving the idea into the mainstream with over 2.6 million monthly readers. They give advice and guidance on making smart choices simple enough for the novice to the eco-savvy. Feature articles range from the environment, business, culture, travel, science, home & garden, eco-design, sustainable fashion and more. Their core promises 'report with integrity, never preach, trust science, refuse green washing...and welcome everyone!'

TRAVEL+ LEISURE

Travel + Leisure
http://www.travelandleisure.com/

A global iconic luxury travel brand for over 50 years, Travel + Leisure has been covering the art of travel from food & wine, to fashion, hotels, destinations, shopping, hiking, skiing and more. Their mission is to inspire and inform, their goal is to help the reader make the most out of their valuable time from travel to transforming leisure at home. They have an extensive collection of feature stories on sustainable travel from shopping to top destinations, to people changing the way we think about sustainability.

The Nature Conservancy Magazine
http://www.treehugger.com/

The Nature Conservancy is a distinguished global environmental organization that brings together scientists, citizens, and leaders to address the pressing issues of climate change and biodiversity loss. Through science-driven, equitable, and collaborative conservation efforts in 81 countires, the organization undertakes initiatives such as volunteer citizen science programs to achieve its goals. Their award-winning magazine combines reporting with world-class photography.

Emergence Magazine
https://emergencemagazine.org/

Emergence Magazine, established in 2018, is an award-winning publication and creative studio that has garnered numerous awards. It delves into the intricate connections between ecology, culture, and spirituality through a diverse array of storytelling and artistic expressions including stories about travel. The magazine employs various mediums, including an annual tactile print edition, which features essays, interviews, poems, artwork, and photo essays. These elements collectively underscore humanity's interdependence with the living Earth. The weekly podcast features author-narrated essays.

S&K
DIGGING DEEPER

DIGGING DEEPER
NON-PROFITS – FOUNDATIONS - INSTITUTIONS

The travel industry is one of the largest service industries globally, significantly contributing to the economy and employing millions of people. The goal of sustainable tourism is to minimize the negative impacts of tourism on the environment. Sustainable tourism practices include using resources responsibly, reducing over-consumption eliminating waste, preserving biodiversity, protecting native wildlife, and creating long-term socio-economic benefits for local communities.

This section of the directory highlights the heroic efforts of non-profits, foundations, and institutions working towards kinder more sustainable tourism, hopefully it will give you a sense of the bigger picture and inspire a deeper dive!

Best Tourism Village (WTO)
https://tourism-villages.unwto.org/

"What is the *Best Tourism Villages* by UN Tourism Initiative? A global initiative to highlight those villages where tourism preserves cultures and traditions, celebrates diversity, provides opportunities and safeguards biodiversity. *UN Tourism is the United Nations* agency responsible for the promotion of responsible, sustainable and universally accessible tourism. UN Tourism promotes tourism as a driver of economic growth, inclusive development and environmental sustainability." A few key points: reduce economic inequality, fight rural depopulation, gender equality, education and skills development, governance, food systems, cultural heritage and reduce waste .

Global Sustainable Tourism Council
http://www.gstcouncil.org/

"*The Global Sustainable Tourism Council (GSTC®) is managing the GSTC* Criteria, global standards for sustainable travel and tourism; as well as providing international accreditation for sustainable tourism Certification Bodies. The *GSTC* is an independent and neutral organization, legally registered in the USA as a 501(c)3 non-profit organization that represents a diverse and global membership, including national and provincial governments, leading travel companies, hotels, tour operators, NGO's, individuals and communities – all striving to achieve best practices in sustainable tourism. Their mission is to be an agent of change in the world of sustainable travel and tourism by fostering the increased knowledge, understanding, adoption and demand for sustainable tourism practices."

Green Destinations
http://www.greendestination.org/

"Green Destinations is a global organization that supports sustainable green destination community. Launched at ITB Berlin 2015, our *Green Destinations Community* features a strong nexus of our representatives, partners, and ambassadors from around the globe, who strive to make tourism better and more sustainable. Every year, *Green Destinations* offers exceptional opportunities for tourism stakeholders to comprehensively discuss sustainable destination management practices and connect with like-minded pioneers and advocates at *Green Destinations Events.* Our signature, biannual events are the *Green Destinations* Story Awards Ceremony at ITB Berlin and the Green Destinations Conference."

DESTINATION COMMUNITY

Leave No Trace
https://lnt.org/

PUBLIC & PRIVATE COMMUNITY

The highly awarded *Leave No Trace* "pioneers science and provides proven, research-based solutions for the protection of the natural world. The organization accomplishes its mission by providing innovative education, skills, research and science to help people care for the outdoors. By working with the public and those managing public lands, *Leave No Trace* focuses on educating people—instead of costly restoration programs or access restrictions—as the most effective and least resource-intensive solution to land protection.Three decades ago, driven by a shared commitment to preserving our natural lands, environmental advocates from the public, the outdoor industry and the land management community came together to form an organization to better protect the outdoors." *Featured in CNN, Forbes, and Outside.*

Planeta.com
https://planeta.com

"*Planeta* pioneers online reporting focusing on conservation and tourism around the globe. What we learned, we shared. What we had questions about, we asked questions about. The result: an award-winning site geared toward conscious travelers, hosts, and everyone in between seeking practical suggestions in the realm of eco-friendly, people-friendly, and place-friendly travel. *Planeta* spotlights local conservation and tourism connections around the globe. We have focused our work connecting the natural and online worlds for nearly 30 years. For independent travelers, we provide practical suggestions in the realm of conscious, eco-friendly, people-friendly, and place-friendly travel. For locals, we amplify and like / share / retweet / embed post showing your work and passions. We also provide workshops and tipsheets showing how to make the most of the social web and old-fashioned analog media."

Sustainable Travel International
https://sustainabletravel.org

"At *Sustainable Travel International,* we believe that people's inherent wanderlust, their desire for new experiences and concern for the places they care for most can inspire the protection of the world's natural and cultural bounty and generate economic opportunity in tourism destinations. Since 2002, we have been charting a new course for travel and tourism — one that leads to a healthier environment, greater economic opportunity, social justice and the protection of natural and cultural resources. We collaborate with local communities, companies, governments, and travelers to achieve the right balance and create a better path forward for some of the most vulnerable destinations around the world. We're working towards a more sustainable future – one characterized by clean beaches, protected parks, climate stability, economic justice, and heritage preservation. Our inclusive and innovative methodologies build knowledge, inspire action, and enable choices that help achieve the UN Sustainable Development Goals." *Featured in HuffPost, Business Insider, and Condé Nast Traveler.*

The Center for Reponsible Travel
http://www.responsibletravel.org/

"The Center for Responsible Travel (CREST) is a globally recognized nonprofit organization dedicated to transforming the way the world travels. Based in Washington, DC but with an international scope, *CREST* provides solutions, resources, and support to governments, policymakers, tourism businesses, and nonprofit organizations to confront tourism's most pressing issues. Our mission is to be a center of tourism knowledge, empowerment, and action for destination communities, and positive change begins with collective action. As a community-driven organization, we believe that every individual has the power to make a difference, and together, we can create a brighter future for all."

 THE CONSCIOUS
TRAVEL FOUNDATION

The Counscious Travel Foundation
http://www.theconscioustravelfoundation.com/

"*The Conscious Travel Foundation* collaborates, educates, advocates and works as a "community think tank and a conduit to industry experts and innovators, helping our members increase their positive impact on landscapes, wildlife, cultures and communities across the globe." Members are a across section of the industry "from hotels, lodges and DMCs, to travel designers, tour operators, guides, PR and marketing businesses and media." The Conscious Travel Foundation provides educational content and contacts that empowers members to make changes in their businesses and destinations from carbon budgets to supply chain management, training and certification. "Philanthropy is a key tenet of *The Conscious Travel Foundation;* membership fees are donated directly to carefully chosen projects linked to tourism." *Featured in Condé Nast Traveller, National Geographic, Forbes, The Telegraph, The Guardian and more.*

The Global Ecotourism Network
http://www.globalecotourismnetwork.org/

"We are a global group of ecotourism pioneers and practitioners, who want to share our many years of experience in ecotourism and sustainable tourism practices and also our wide contact network to help others. We love nature, innovation and sustainable design, different cultures, great guides and know how important sustainability is for sharing a liveable planet. We are represented in 99 countries and 6 global regions, which are setting up their own networks, linking into the Global one." *GEN* facilitates a community-based website that shares best practices, research, innovation and events. They assist in campaigns, technical visits, conferences on ecotourism, conservation and community.

The International Ecotourism Society (TIES)
https://ecotourism.org/

"*The International Ecotourism Society (TIES)* is a nonprofit organization dedicated to promoting ecotourism. Founded in 1990, *TIES* has been on the forefront of the development of ecotourism, providing guidelines and standards, training, technical assistance, and educational resources. *TIES*' global network of ecotourism professionals and travelers is leading the efforts to make tourism a viable tool for conservation, protection of bio-cultural diversity, and sustainable community development. Through membership services, industry outreach and educational programs, *TIES* is committed to helping organizations, communities and individuals promote and practice the principles of ecotourism. *TIES* currently has members in more than 190 countries and territories, representing various professional fields and industry segments including: academics, consultants, conservation professionals and organizations, governments, architects, tour operators, lodge owners and managers, general development experts, and ecotourists."

Tourism Cares
http://www.tourismcares.org/

"*Tourism Cares* is committed to promoting sustainable tourism and implementing policies that support environmental, social, and economic well-being into all of our programs. Our initiatives are designed to inspire and educate our members, helping them adopt sustainable practices in their operations. By aligning our efforts with the *United Nations Sustainable Development Goals (SDGs)*, we aim to create a positive impact on local communities, ecosystems, and the global tourism sector. *Tourism Cares* is a 501(c)(3) U.S.-based global non-profit that is dedicated to advancing the travel industry's positive social, environmental, and economic impact to help people and places thrive. We drive positive impact through our mission-driven programming - support local communities, address environmental impact, preserve social and cultural heritage, enhance visitor experience and education."

UN World Tourism Organization (WTO)
https://unwto.org/

"*The World Tourism Organization (UNWTO)* enters a new era today with a new name and brand: *UN Tourism*. With this new brand, the Organization reaffirms its status as the *United Nations* specialized agency for tourism and the global leader of tourism for development, driving social and economic change to ensure that "people and planet" are always center stage. As society progresses, the tourism sector, much like many other sectors, needs to transform to serve as a catalyst for prosperity at a universal scale. Enhancing the well-being of individuals, safeguarding the natural environment, stimulating economic advancement, and fostering international harmony are key goals that are the fundamental essence of *UN Tourism*. The organization takes on the role of driving a sustainable force that is now central to many economies."

World Travel Tourism Council
https://wttc.org/

"For over 30 years, *WTTC* has conducted research on the economic impact of Travel & Tourism in 185 countries and issues such as overcrowding, taxation, policy-making, and many others to raise awareness of the importance of the Travel & Tourism sector as one of the world's largest economic sectors. As a non-profit membership-based organization, our members and partners are the core of our organization and include over 200 CEOs, Chairpersons, and Presidents of the world's leading Travel & Tourism companies from all geographies and industries. *WTTC* promotes sustainable growth for the Travel & Tourism sector, working with governments and international institutions to create jobs, drive exports and generate prosperity."

World Wide Opportunities on Organic Farms (WWOOF)
https://wwoof.net

WWOOF is a non-profit movement made up of people that are passionate about sustainability and regenerative farming. With 53 years and over 130 countries, *WWOOF* provides you with a way to learn about organic farming, agriculture, and build a global community of ecological farming practices. You'll gain skills, experience rural living, and immersive yourself in another culture. How does it work? "*WWOOFers* step into the daily life of their host family to learn about agro-ecological and sustainable farming methods through hands-on experience. Hosts offer accommodation and meals with no money exchanged between hosts and *WWOOFers*."

Ecotourism World
https://ecotourism-world.com/about-us/

Ecotourism World is an *information platform* committed to the promotion of ecotourism and sustainable travel. It aims to inform and inspire travelers to make environmentally responsible choices that not only enrich their travel experience but also contribute to making sustainable travel the global standard. They also offer an intern program that offers skill-building work experiences in sustainable travel. Ecotourism World became a media partner with Asia Ecotourism Network (AEN) in July 2020.

The Travel Foundation
https://www.thetravelfoundation.org.uk

The Travel Foundation, a highly regarded international organization dedicated to sustainable tourism, was established in 2003. Operating across 36 countries, the foundation is committed to promoting tourism models that harmonize the needs of local communities with environmental conservation. This is achieved through rigorous research, comprehensive training programs, and dedicated mentoring initiatives.

S&K
SUSTAINABLE
PACKER

S&K RECOMMENDED PRODUCTS FOR THE
"SUSTAINABLE PACKER"

This section of the directory features businesses committed to creating sustainable, innovative and beautifully designed products for the traveler, from camper to mountain climber and yes, the homebody too! The founders and creators of these companies are experienced travelers and entrepreneurs who have created mission driven businesses because of their commitment to saving our plant for future generations!

The businesses featured are part of a fast growing and inspiring global movement towards a more sustainable future in the use of groundbreaking technology and design using nature-based, upcycled or recycled materials. Many companies are also focused on eliminating single-use plastics to getting plastics out of our seas, planting trees, or supporting local communities.

The majority of the companies recommended are committed to one or more certifying organizations (although there are other certifying bodies not shown):

1% for the Planet members commit to donating at least 1% of annual sales directly to environmental organizations. We certify every donation to ensure businesses meet that commitment

All certified companies must meet the same high standard for climate accountability by adopting a standardized carbon fee and actively funding projects that reduce emissions.

Anchal
https://anchalproject.org/

"Anchal is a non-profit social enterprise that leverages design and collaboration to create sustainable, income-generating careers in eco-friendly textiles for marginalized women in India. Our *Fair Trade-verified*, eco-friendly travel accessories are the perfect solution for long weekend trips and much-needed vacations. Choose from canvas duffle bags, travel organizers, large toiletry bags, and roomy canvas totes to meet all your storage needs. With spacious compartments and made from sustainable materials like 100% organic cotton and upcycled vintage cotton, these travel bags ensure you're well-prepared for your next journey!"

Bellyroy
http://www.bellroy.com/

"We believe business can be a force for good in the world, and we're working hard to create a more vibrant future. We're proud to be part of the B Corp movement, in which certified companies use the power of business to help solve social and environmental problems. We are committed to making them more environmentally sustainable – using fabrics made from recycled and plant-derived materials, and sourcing leathers with the least environmental impact. The 100% recycled polyester and nylon fabrics we use in our bags and pouches perform just as well as virgin materials, with far less impact on the environment.."

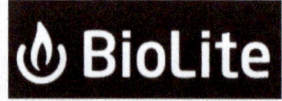

POWER - LIGHT - COOKING

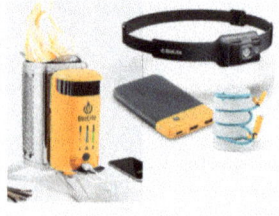

"We are on a mission to empower people & protect our planet through access to renewable energy. The planet's future will be shared by all of us - and we're here to make that future bright for everyone. Our vision is to provide 20 million people with access to clean energy and to avoid 3 million tons of CO_2e by the year 2025. BioLite creates affordable, durable products that harness surrounding energy to cook, charge, and light daily life for off-grid households. Headquartered in Nairobi Kenya, the BioLite Emerging Markets (EM) Team works closely with key partners across 23 countries to provide last-mile distribution, training, and financing to remote customers."

BAGS - BAMBOO UTENSILS

ChicoBag & To-Go Ware
http://www.chicobag.com/

"Misson: Help humanity bag the single-use habit. As leaders in cutting-edge corporate sustainability, *ChicoBag* and *To-Go Ware* are committed to protecting our planet from pollution and preserving its beauty for generations to come. We create high quality, long-lasting reusable bags, cutlery, and containers. We hope humanity will exchange their single-use products for these eco-friendly options that won't live in the ocean or landfill for thousands of years. Rigorous safety and contaminant testing, certified recycled yarn, fair labor rules, ethical manufacturing, high quality and extreme durability, zero-waste operations—these are just a few of the ways we hold ourselves accountable as a responsible manufacturer, business partner, and retailer. "

Carry Courage
https://carrycourage.com/

"We exist to create and inspire a community of courageous women to make a positive impact on the planet through sustainable choices and transparency of our process. Carry Courage takes a restorative approach in our business and values living out circular design ideals. We seek out fair labor practices, earth conscious materials (like cork fabric and linen) and hand craft them into beautiful, functional products without compromise. Through our intentional efforts now, our vision is to become a confidence building catalyst for women around the world, as well as contribute to a world that values humans and our connection to the environment."

Bellyroy
http://www.cotopaxi.com/

"Adventure inspires us to see the world and make it better. That's why we create responsibly made outdoor gear that brings performance, color, and joy to all, and helps us build a movement to support communities around the world. We support people impacted by poverty around the world, with a primary focus on Latin America. We dedicate 1% of annual revenue to the Cotopaxi Foundation, which supports nonprofits with proven track records of reducing poverty through health care, education, and livelihoods. We approach sustainability holistically. Since our biggest impacts occur within our supply chain, we work with factories that prioritize sustainability and treat workers right. We also choose recycled, leftover deadstock, and other sustainably minded materials for over 96% of our products."

 **EarthHero**

"By shopping on *EarthHero*, you're helping to build a more sustainable world. We take our responsibility to make the planet better seriously, and these certifications are just one example of that commitment. From public transparency to environmental performance (and so much more), being a B Corp means we're working alongside a network of companies looking to redefine what success in business really means. Businesses awarded the B Corp title have met the highest standards of social and environmental performance, public transparency, and legal accountability. "

Goal Zero
https://goalzero.com/

"We've been inspired by a passion for innovation, respect for the planet, and a humanitarian heart. *Goal Zero* isn't just a company, it's a business created by people who live life to the fullest. Inspired by passion for adventure, respect for the planet, and a humanitarian heart - we take both our work and our play seriously and are proud to provide the most innovative solar products on the market to empower people with a safe, connected, and sustainable future by delivering accessible energy resilience and solutions for home and away. "

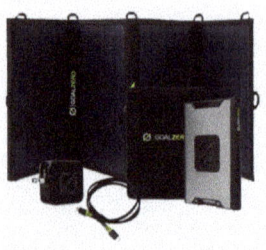

Hibear
http://www.hibear.co/

"... there is nothing more frustrating than trash in our wild places. We are committed to be part of that solution. We offset our own impact and give back to the outdoor community. Hibear is both Climate Neutral Certified and a 1% for the Planet member company. After traveling 'round the world we learned the value of less and that the things we carry should do more. Hibear has a strong commitment to sustainability and being part of the climate change solution. As an outdoor brand, we are at the forefront of these initiatives. We believe the products we create have a direct and profound impact on reducing the amount of trash in our landfills and oceans. All of our packaging and products are delivered with recyclable and thoughtfully crafted reusable materials."

Hydro Flask
http://www.hydroflask.com/

"Adventure inspires us to see the world and make it better. That's why we create responsibly made outdoor gear that brings performance, color, and joy to all, and helps us build a movement to support communities around the world. We support people impacted by poverty around the world, with a primary focus on Latin America. We dedicate 1% of annual revenue to the Cotopaxi Foundation, which supports nonprofits with proven track records of reducing poverty through health care, education, and livelihoods. We approach sustainability holistically. Since our biggest impacts occur within our supply chain, we work with factories that prioritize sustainability and treat workers right. We also choose recycled, leftover deadstock, and other sustainably minded materials for over 96% of our products."

Klean Kanteen
http://www.kleankanteen.com/

"In 2004 we kicked off the Bring *Your Own*™ revolution by offering the first reusable stainless steel water bottles in the United States.Back in the early 2000s, the popularity of bottled water was on the rise. Suddenly, everyone seemed to be sipping from single-use plastic bottles as they went about their days. At the time, few people understood the human health risks of plastic or could foresee just how many of those plastic bottles would end up littering the planet. Today our company continues to revolutionize reusables by making them more sustainable, durable, and functional than ever before."

CONTAINERS & CANTEENS

Lifestraw
http://www.lifestraw.com/

LifeStraw

DRINK SAFE WATER

"At *LifeStraw*, we recognize the undeniable intersection between the impact that we as a company have on the climate, the disproportionate impact that climate change has on many of the communities that we support, and our responsibility to protect and advocate for a healthier planet. We strive to create products from sustainable materials that offer healthy alternatives to more wasteful options such as single-use plastics. We also create sustainable packaging that avoids use of plastic and maximizes recyclability and composability. We are a Climate Neutral Certified Brand, measuring and offsetting our annual greenhouse gas emissions. In 2021, we committed to setting science-based targets, to not only offset but reduce our greenhouse gas emissions, even as we grow as a company. We are also active members of the outdoor industry and global community's fight against climate change through our membership in and partnership with various climate advocacy and policy organizations."

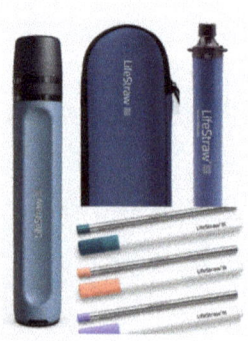

Marley
http://www.thehouseofmarley.com/

M A R L E Y

"House of Marley is built on the principles of superior quality, sustainability and a commitment to charitable causes. We are driven to enhance lives through great product experiences as well as using proceeds from product sales to support global reforestation through Project Marley. *House of Marley's* eco-conscious identity was created in collaboration with the Marley family to carry on Bob Marley's legacy of love for music and planet. *House of Marley's* Eco-Friendly Speakers are crafted from bamboo, recyclable aluminum, recycled plastic, and our sustainable REWIND® fabric and REGRIND® silicone and cork; our Bluetooth speakers blend top-notch sound with environmental consciousness. Elevate your music experience while making a positive impact on the planet."

nomadix◇

Nomadix
http://www.nomadix.co/

"Sustainability is woven into who we are and what we make. That's why we are committed to reducing our impact on the planet by creating durable and versatile products, using recycled materials, manufacturing responsibly, and collaborating for change. Millions of plastic bottles recycled and counting. Our commitment to the environment begins with repurposing post-consumer recycled materials to make all of our products. Those recycled materials are transformed into premium fibers durable enough to hang with you through any adventure so you can own less and do more. Nomadix understands the importance of coming together to better our planet. "

"...we focus on creating gear reviews, guides, packing lists, and other content to help you travel smarter and more efficiently. Through honest reviews that incorporate real world testing and an excruciating attention to detail, our goal is to cut through marketing jargon to give you the nitty-gritty stuff you need to know. Our Process: A small team of travel experts test and review a variety of premium and economical gear in their element for a minimum of two weeks. The output is an honest, objective review. We'll never accept cash or allow free gear to influence a review. Ever. While we strive for variety, we do believe in paying more for something that will last. And prefer brands with a good, ethical production process at a price point that makes sense for its lifeline."

MULTI SOURCED GEAR

SUSTAINABLE LUGGAGE - BAGS

Paravel
https://tourparavel.com/

PARAVEL

"We are a travel-inspired brand with sustainability at the core of everything we do. We believe travel can be transformative and celebrate all forms, local and far - from a trip to the park to a milestone life celebration on the other side of the world. We create impeccably designed, multi-functional, sustainable bags, luggage and accessories: companions for all journeys. 100% of our products use recycled and upcycled materials. We obsess over design, function and quality and consider every detail to use best-in-class recycled materials and components wherever possible. We have been certifiedby Climate Neutral since 2021, a nonprofit organization that works to decrease global greenhouse gas emissions. We commit to and achieve the industry-leading benchmark for brand wide carbon-neutrality."

Pategonia
http://www.patagonia.com/

"At *Patagonia*, we appreciate that all life on earth is under threat of extinction. We're using the resources we have—our business, our investments, our voice and our imaginations—to do something about it. ACTIVISIM: We're Taxing Ourselves - *Patagonia*'s self-imposed Earth tax, 1% for the Planet, provides support to environmental nonprofits working to defend our air, land and water around the globe. We're Linking Sports with Activism - Our Global Sport Activist® employees are using their roles in the sport community to drive positive social and environmental change. Connect with Environmental Groups - We're connecting individuals with *Patagonia* grantees, to take action on the most pressing issues facing the world today. *Patagonia Action Works* helps you discover events, petitions and skilled volunteering opportunities in your backyard and donate money to local causes. Explore Activism Stories - Discover the most pressing stories from environmental protectors across the world."

saalt

Saalt's
https://saalt.com/

"Toxin-laden, single-use disposable products are harming our bodies and polluting our planet. We deserve better. That's why we create premium, reusable products that are healthy for our bodies and the environment without sacrificing comfort and performance. And we give 1% back to help end global poverty in the process. As a certified B Corp, we give 1% to donate period care to regions with the most need, and help fund initiatives in menstrual health, girls' education, and sustainability. Since our launch in 2018, we've donated over 100,000 Saalt products to women and girls in need in 50 countries."

Scrubba Portable Wash Bag
https://thescrubba.com/

"In addition to making innovative products to make your journey easier, Scrubba by Calibre8 is committed to responsible environmental and social practices. We use quality materials to ensure a long product lifespan and design our products to be easily repairable. We're proud to announce that we've officially been Climate Neutral Certified. In 2022 we formally partnered with 1% for the Planet, committing to donating 1% of our total revenue each year to environmental causes. By using minimal water and no electricity, each Scrubba wash bag saves travellers an average of 1000 liters of water and 7.5kg of carbon each year. By using your Scrubba wash bag you are minimizing your travel footprint."

Solgaard Lifepack
https://solgaard.co/

SOLGAARD

"Design driven and always ready for adventure. We enhance life on-the-go with premium gear for global citizens. We believe in intentional, sustainable design. We produce products that improve travel life that don't damage our planet. Climate positive going beyond neutral. We inspire people to explore everything the world has to offer. Our only mandate is that we give more than we take. For every item sold, we save 6 lbs. of ocean-bound plastic from coastal communities. We've partnered with different groups in The Philippines, Indonesia, and China who work with local teams in creating jobs for communities to collect ocean-bound plastic that can be upcycled into useful goods. "

Suds & Eco
https://suds.eco/

Suds & Eco is plastic free , zero waste, cruelty free, palm oil free, and ethically handmade - made better for you, home, and planet. "Sustainably sourced with all-natural ingredients, teeming with organic nourishment that hair loves, each bar is a masterpiece of Mother Nature's making. Beautifully boxed with the minimalist in mind, each bar comes completely packaged in biodegradable & compostable materials." *Featured in People Magazine, Buzzfeed, HuffPost and more.*

Sustainable Travel & Living Store
http://www.sustainabletravelandliving.com/

"Each year, 1.4 billion of us wanderlust warriors are traveling around this globe we call home. That equals great power: to leave less waste, to create and share good habits, to support the cultures and communities we've come to experience and, where we can, to leave each place just a little better than we found it.

We've put together an awesome collection of gear and great info to help you do just that. One we hope that, just as travel forever changes the lens through which you see the world, might better our actions in all areas of life. Every dollar you spend casts a vote for the world you want to live in. The reality is, nothing we do is going to be perfect. But if we each make better choices one step at a time, it adds up to big impacts."

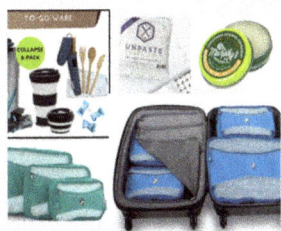

 VOITED

"Our mission is to create unique, eco-friendly outdoor products that are purposeful and inspire us to get out there. By combining our love for the outdoors with our dedication to lessen the impact that manufacturing has on the environment, we create collections that blend creativity, performance, quality, and value. We integrate only the best eco-conscious materials with the most useful features and we design with multiple purposes, high functionality and sustainability in mind. Our lightweight, durable, and packable outdoor products are equipped with useful details to save you time and space so that you can purely enjoy your adventures. We have worked very hard to achieve such sustainable and responsible practices. It's a project shared between the people who make our products and those responsible for *VOITED*. We are continually striving for zero waste and zero impact on the environment."

BLANKETS - OUTERWEAR - PONCHOS

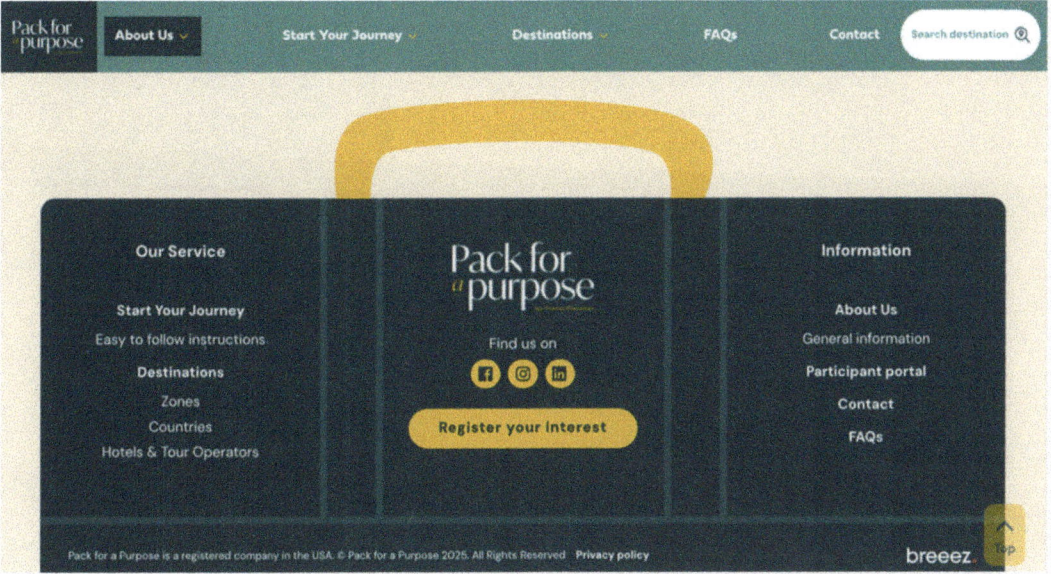

PACK FOR A PURPOSE MISSION

"Connecting travelers with in-destination service providers who deliver purposely packed donations to local communities around the globe. There is much need around the world, especially in popular travel destinations. And there are many travelers who want to make a meaningful contribution to the locations they visit.

Our goal is to connect travelers with community projects where they visit. This is the genesis of how Pack for a Purpose was started by emeritus founder, Rebecca Rothney in 2010. A global initiative that encourages travelers to make a meaningful contribution to the communities they visit by dedicating a small space in their luggage to essential supplies.

Travel Elevates, a non-profit foundation that leverages global travel partnerships to help build sustainable communities in much traveled destinations. We are happy to no have Pack for a Purpose under our foundation umbrella. We proudly offer Pack for a Purpose as a main resource to our travel advisors and travelers worldwide.

Our Impact:Last year Pack for a Purpose travelers packed **8,400 suitcases** with **21 tons (42,000 lbs.)** of essential supplies. That is equivalent to the entire weight of a commercial jet. The results show that small spaces and little effort really does bring a big impact!"

https://www.packforapurpose.org/about-us/

The Nature Conservancy

In order to offset the carbon footprint of the printed and eBook versions of the S & K Directory, a portion of sales will be donated to The Nature Conservancy's Plant a Billion Trees campaign. www.nature.org

PLANT A BILLION TREES

"The Nature Conservancy's Plant a Billion Trees campaign is a major forest restoration program. Our goal is to restore forests across the planet to help people and slow the connected crises of climate change and biodiversity loss."

www.ingramcontent.com/pod-product-compliance
Lightning Source LLC
Chambersburg PA
CBHW041141120626
46547CB00020B/3065